Multinational Corporations and U.N. Politics

Pergamon Policy Studies on U.S. and International Business

Related Titles

PERGAMON
POLICY
STUDIES

ON U.S. AND
INTERNATIONAL BUSINESS

Multinational Corporations and U.N. Politics
The Quest for Codes of Conduct

Werner J. Feld

Pergamon Press

NEW YORK • OXFORD • TORONTO • SYDNEY • FRANKFURT • PARIS

Pergamon Press Offices:

U.S.A.	Pergamon Press Inc., Maxwell House, Fairview Park, Elmsford, New York 10523, U.S.A.
U.K.	Pergamon Press Ltd., Headington Hill Hall, Oxford OX3 0BW, England
CANADA	Pergamon of Canada, Ltd., 150 Consumers Road, Willowdale, Ontario M2J, 1P9, Canada
AUSTRALIA	Pergamon Press (Aust) Pty. Ltd., P O Box 544, Potts Point, NSW 2011, Australia
FRANCE	Pergamon Press SARL, 24 rue des Ecoles, 75240 Paris, Cedex 05, France
FEDERAL REPUBLIC OF GERMANY	Pergamon Press GmbH, 6242 Kronberg/Taunus, Pferdstrasse 1, Federal Republic of Germany

Copyright © 1980 Pergamon Press Inc.

Library of Congress Cataloging in Publication Data

Feld, Werner J
  Multinational corporations and U.N. politics.

  (Pergamon policy studies)
  Bibliography: p.
  Includes index.
  1. Underdeveloped areas—International business enterprises. 2. United Nations. 3. Industry and state. I. Title. II. Title: Codes of conduct.
HD2755.5.F44 1979   338.8'8   79-18654
ISBN 0-08-022488-1

Printed in the United States of America
Second Printing 1981

Contents

List of Tables
and Figures

vii

Preface

The completion of this study has been slower than anticipated because the negotiations regarding codes of conduct for multinational corporations proceeding in several United Nations forum have lagged behind the original timetables. Of course, this is not really surprising considering the wide gap in the initial positions on the part of the main antagonists in these negotiations, the Group of "77" and the Western industrialized countries. Nevertheless, substantial progress has been made since 1975 to bridge this gap although some issues still await final resolution. The progress made so far provides us not only with an interesting general overview as to what the substantive features of the codes are likely to be, but also makes it possible to assess this drawn-out process to reach compromises on various issues that perhaps are not fully satisfactory to many, yet offer acceptable solutions. Moreover, the negotiating process offers valuable insights into the political climate pervading the efforts of the Third World to bring about changes in the existing economic system and to introduce gradually the New International Economic Order.

This study could not have been accomplished without the help of a number of people. My special thanks go to Richard J. Smith, Michael Boerner, and Elinor G. Constable, all with the Department of State, for providing some insight into the thinking of responsible United States officials on the code problems. I would also like to express my sincere gratitude to Karl P. Sauvant and Boris Velic' of the Centre for Transnational Corporations for making available to me valuable documentation on the negotiating process for the code. Finally, I would like to thank Glenda Wingard for typing part of the first draft of the manuscript and last, but certainly not least, I am most grateful to Jan Davis for typing the final version of the manuscript and for her superb editorial assistance.

1 The Power of MNCs: Third World Concerns and Strategies

During the last decade, the multinational corporations (MNCs) have become increasingly a subject of controversy. While the academic treatment of MNCs used to be mostly the domain of business-administration specialists and economists, scholars in other disciplines, especially political science, have turned their attention to the impact MNCs have had and continue to have on national government decision making and on the international system. There is little doubt that the immense economic power and financial muscle of MNCs have presented an enormous challenge to the sovereignty of governments of large and small states alike, but the specific effects that these mammoth private actors may have on the existing international economic and political systems are far from clear and remain a matter of intense argument, as is evident from the scrutiny of the large number of studies undertaken up to now. (1)

As used in this volume, the term "multinational corporation" is understood in a broad sense and includes private, state-owned, and mixed enterprises. Each enterprise carries out various economic functions such as production, marketing, and research in different countries simultaneously, with resources being allocated without regard to national frontiers. Its affiliates (branches, subsidiaries, joint ventures) are joined together by ties of common ownership or various means of control and are responsive to an overall common management strategy. (2)

More recently the term "transnational corporation" has become popular when referring to MNCs because it is used in United Nations studies and proceedings since the establishment of the Commission on Transnational Corporations by the United Nations Economic and Social Council in 1975. However, this term focuses attention mainly on the relations between the enterprise and its affiliates (as well as among the affiliates themselves) and fails to address the key notion of these entities, which is economic activity of <u>one</u> enterprise in a multitude of

1

nation-states.   Therefore, I prefer to use the traditional term of multinational corporation in this book and consider it synonymous with "transnational corporation" whenever that term is used in United Nations documents and organizations.

To place the MNC in perspective, a few figures are useful. In 1977, General Motors, the largest MNC in the world at present, produced goods and services totalling $55 billion. If this figure is compared with the data on the Gross National Product (GNP) of the world's 150-odd nation-states, General Motors would rank 20th from the top, ahead of Switzerland and behind Belgium.   Indeed, 500 MNCs headquartered mainly in the United States, Western Europe, and Japan produce goods and services in excess of $1 billion. (3)   Only about half of the nation-states are able to equal or surpass this record.   Another startling MNC dimension is employment. General Motors has about 800,000 employees around the world, more than the total civil service of New Zealand. Some observers have suggested that, by the end of the 1980s, 20 percent of the globe's labor force might be employed by a relatively small number of 300 very powerful MNCs that would control a large part of world production. (4)

American and European giant firms such as Unilever, IBM, Nestle, Exxon, or Philips are able to obtain capital from anywhere in the world if they need it, although many of these giants not only generate sufficient revenue to be self-financing, but also on occasion lend money to banks.   Moreover, these large MNCs have developed worldwide production-distribution systems that make it possible to launch new products anywhere in the world and reach millions of customers all over the globe. They have the financial resources to undertake research and development activities necessary to make and exploit breakthroughs in science and technology.   They can diversify their risks by global investment patterns, reducing their vulnerability to the economic and political cycles of a given state and by takeovers or acquisition moves by other companies.

COPING WITH THE MNC

While the governments of both developed and developing countries have to cope with the enormous power of MNCs, the problems as perceived by the governmental leaders of the two types of countries differ in substance and intensity. Moreover, the political conditions under which governmental policy responses are given to MNC challenges also vary. In both cases, the basic issue is to weigh the economic benefits that may be derived from the operations of MNCs in a particular country against economic and social policy, autonomy, and security concerns. In industrialized democracies, this also means efforts to reconcile con-flicting interests of various domestic groups that might be affected by the current or prospective activities of MNCs. All this can produce serious internal and external strains, as governmental actions in France against potential takeovers of French electronics firms in the 1960s (5) as well as recurrent Canadian displeasure with United States domination of many of their industries (6) have demonstrated. Of course, in developed countries with representative governmental systems, the MNC or its subsidiary can participate in the political process and can press its interests in the legislative and administrative councils. On the other hand, governments in these countries usually possess the analytical and administrative expertise to evaluate current and proposed MNC activities in terms of benefits and costs related to broad governmental goals and programs. As a result, relevant controls can be administered in most cases to assure acceptable MNC behavior without stultifying the corporations' pursuit of legitimate economic objectives.

These problems are much more complex in the developing world. In the first place, the economic power asymmetry between MNCs and most of these countries is awesome and produces great, and generally justified, anxieties regarding their governmental autonomy of policy choices. Since the political leadership in many Third World countries (7) remains preoccupied with nation-building, any potential impairment of sovereignty is perceived as a threat to this process by the leaders and the general public alike. In addition, the political leadership may well fear that its position of authority and prestige could be undermined.

Secondly, indigenous enterprises are not eager to see the establishment of competing MNC subsidiaries, which might produce better, yet lower-priced goods, and whose economic strength might be able to preempt the loan resources of local banks, thereby severely reducing their own borrowing opportunities. Hence, pressures are exerted on the national governments to oppose the entry of new MNC subsidiaries.

Thirdly, the majority of developing countries lack the governmental experts to negotiate with the highly sophisticated representatives of MNCs either to bargain out an agreement on the establishment of a new subsidiary or to set up effective mechanisms to control MNC behavior that will not kill the "golden goose."

Considering the MNCs' well-known capability for transfer-pricing, which allows them to manipulate profits across national boundaries and take them in a subsidiary located in a country with the lowest tax system, and their ability to withhold technologies that might be badly needed by the indigenous government, it is obvious that such negotiations require a high level of skill on the part of the government representatives. Meanwhile, the less developed countries (LDCs) have imposed various limiting measures on MNC subsidiaries, including special taxes, ceilings on license fees paid to MNC headquarters, restrictions on the use of local credits, and others.

These factors have placed many Third World countries in a difficult dilemma: they need the economic, technological, financial, and managerial resources MNCs have to offer, but they fear that the political cost of taking advantage of these resources is too great. The consequence has been a high degree of tension and friction between developing countries and MNCs, many of which begin to reconsider the need of establishing new subsidiaries in the Third World or, in fact, wonder whether it is worthwhile to continue their operations there. This situation has been caused to a large extent by the growing interdependence of the world's economics and aggravated by the spreading network of manifold relations and interactions created by the MNCs themselves.

INTERDEPENDENCY AND DEPENDENCY

During the last few years, the term "interdependence" has become an "in" word. Secretary of State Kissinger used the term with increasing frequency, and in July 1975 the United States Department of State issued a special 30-page report entitled "Toward a Strategy of Interdependence." (8) It has been asserted that the consequences of interdependence could well be constraints on both business enterprises and national governments, inasmuch as decisions disregarding the interdependence relationship or seeking disentanglement could entail considerable cost. (9)   As a result, the attainment of national goals, including national stability, egalitarianism, and effective political participation, may be threatened. Of course, if one assumes that MNCs are creations of a rational world order based upon the true common economic interests of mankind whereby living standards would be raised globally, social disparities reduced, and the gap between private and governmental actors induced by interdependence, then their expansion would be all to the good. But others look upon MNCs as evil spirits that utilize their immense power ruthlessly to reap greater profits and to enhance their power without concern for the welfare of the people, and naturally these observers view growing interdependence brought about by MNCs as a dangerous prospect. (10)

How realistic is the notion that interdependence compels private and governmental actors to make decisions in line with particular existing economic or political transnational relationships?   Some writers are very doubtful about this aspect, (11) and, therefore, it may be useful to clarify the notion of interdependence.

A broad notion of interdependence has been put forth by Oran Young, who defines it as "the extent to which events occurring in any given part or within any given component of a world system affect (either physically or perceptually) events taking place in each of the other parts or component units of the system." (12) Edward L. Morse's definition is also broad and focuses on interdependent behavior that is understood "in terms of the outcome of specified actions of two or more parties (individuals, governments, corporations, etc.) when such actions are mutually contingent." (13) Equally broad, but directed primarily to economics, is Richard N. Cooper's notion which suggests that interdependence is present when there is an increased "sensitivity" to external economic developments. (14)   A more restrictive concept comes from Kenneth Waltz, who focuses on the cost of disentanglement of an interdependent relationship; therefore, a relationship in which one party is merely "affected" by what another does would not necessarily be "interdependence." (15)

All these definitions give few details about the cause-effect relationship of interdependence. Therefore, a more appropriate definition seems to be one advanced by William D. Coplin and Michael K. O'Leary, according to whom interdependence suggests

> the existence of conditions in which the perceived needs of some individual groups in one state are satisfied by the sources or capabilities that exist in at least one other state. Thus patterns of transnational interdependence are a product of the interface between needs and capabilities across national boundaries. (16)

Interdependence is manifested by flows of people, civilian and military goods and services, capital, and information across national boundaries in response to needs in one or more countries in accordance with the capabilities of others. Depending on their particular interests, intergovernmental organizations (IGOs), MNCs, and a variety of governmental and nongovernmental groups such as particular bureaucracies or economic pressure groups may be involved in these flows. The existence of similar needs may lead to formal and informal coalitions among states, among states and IGOs, and among governmental and nongovernmental actors. Complementarity of capabilities may also produce alliances. On the other hand, the unequal distribution of capabilities may conjure up perceptions of dependence by less-favored states, creating apprehension and envy, and possibly leading to friction and conflict. Similar capabilities coupled with unequal resources may sharpen economic competition in international trade and in the search for sources of raw materials.

A distinction has been made by Robert O. Keohane and Joseph S. Nye between sensitivity interdependence and vulnerability interdependence. (17) The former refers generally to the effects of transactions generated by the interface between needs and capabilities across national boundaries on the participants' policies "which become sensitive to one another through the effects of these flows." (18) The second type of interdependence involves the possibility or ability of compelling changes in the relationship between interdependent parties or within the territorial or functional area controlled by a governmental or nongovernmental actor. It also deals with the cost of disentanglement, meaning that the less dependent an actor, the lower the cost of terminating or drastically altering an interdependence relationship. As Keohane and Nye point out, interdependence produces sources of power for some actors and vulnerabilities for others. Strengths and weaknesses vary from issue area to issue area and from one interdependent relationship to another. The raw material sector is an obvious case in point, and the problems of petroleum dependence are well known. The ability to apply countervailing strategies and policies by those governmental or nongovernmental actors who suffer from real or imagined perceptions of dependence in asymmetrical interdependence

situations in one of the crucial questions in an increasingly interdependent world. It is the source of many conflicts that plague the
relationship between MNCs and the Third World, and the resolution of
these conflicts is complex and difficult, especially since a growing
number of political forces has become involved.

The Magnitude of Interdependence

The extent of interdependence existing between MNCs and Third World
countries can be gleaned from two factors: the number of MNC parent
companies and their affiliates in LDCs, and the annual amount of
investments made by the MNCs. Table 1.1 shows that there are 3,502
parent companies in 14 European countries, the United States, Canada,
Japan, Australia, and New Zealand with affiliates in one LDC host
country; and 698 parent companies with affiliates in six or more LDC
host countries. Within the two categories of affiliates, United States
corporations constitute 34.1 and 39.5 percent respectively. It is
interesting to note that the spread of parent companies into developing
countries varies appreciably according to where parent company
headquarters are located. Between 55 and 60 percent of MNCs based in
Australia, Japan, and Portugal have established affiliates in one LDC.
Between 40 and 45 percent of MNCs headquartered in France, Spain,
and the United Kingdom have done so and in the cases of France and the
United Kingdom the relatively high percentage of MNC affiliates in the
developing countries should have been expected in view of their
extensive colonial history.

For the same reason, but in reverse, the percentages of MNC
parents in West Germany, Italy, and New Zealand which have affiliates
in LDCs is much lower (20-35 percent), and those for firms based in the
remainder of the countries listed in table 1.1 are lower yet (13 to 17
percent). This table also indicates that a majority of multinational
operations remain concentrated in the developed countries, but that the
Third World has attracted a substantial number of MNC affiliates.

Table 1.2 breaks the data down further in terms of geographic
distribution and shows that the ties between MNCs and Third World
countries are most intense in Latin America, followed by Asia and
Africa. While the United States has the largest number of multinational
corporations with affiliates in most countries, followed by the United
Kingdom and West Germany, it is not surprising that in Africa, because
of the former colonial ties, the number of affiliates of MNCs based in
the United Kingdom and France appreciably exceed those of American
MNCs.

Although tables 1.1 and 1.2 provide an overview of the linkages and
interdependencies created by the network of MNC affiliates, they do
not say anything about the economic power of the parent companies
located in the various countries listed in the tables. By focusing on
sales figures and the number of employees of the largest MNCs, table
1.3 shows the overwhelming size and strength of American MNCs and

TABLE 1.1. Firms with one or more foreign affiliates, by number of host developing countries with the total of host developed and developing countries in parenthesis (1977)

	Number of parent firms with one or more foreign affiliates in					
	One developing country	Two developing countries	Three developing countries	Four developing countries	Five developing countries	Six or more developing countries
United States of America	1,197 (2,783)	720 (1,608)	525 (1,256)	422 (1,041)	336 (869)	276 (757)
United Kingdom	639 (1,598)	401 (1,005)	313 (747)	264 (581)	219 (474)	187 (398)
Germany, Federal Republic of	316 (1,404)	135 (759)	76 (520)	53 (372)	41 (285)	31 (211)
Switzerland	109 (852)	55 (528)	37 (229)	25 (179)	22 (139)	21 (99)
Netherlands	104 (600)	62 (252)	48 (156)	35 (127)	27 (99)	24 (80)
France	246 (564)	163 (341)	110 (252)	83 (201)	68 (162)	57 (130)
Canada	121 (432)	48 (204)	28 (112)	22 (67)	21 (45)	18 (39)
Japan	225 (380)	126 (210)	85 (158)	60 (127)	49 (94)	41 (77)
Belgium	90 (320)	40 (138)	22 (96)	17 (67)	15 (53)	7 (41)
Australia	181 (323)	82 (176)	48 (108)	32 (70)	17 (50)	10 (39)
Italy	58 (249)	27 (122)	18 (83)	9 (59)	8 (45)	7 (34)
Sweden	63 (258)	39 (165)	31 (124)	20 (102)	17 (86)	14 (75)
New Zealand	58 (167)	10 (51)	5 (20)	3 (11)	2 (7)	- (4)
Denmark	22 (132)	11 (56)	7 (68)	4 (50)	3 (38)	2 (32)
Norway	15 (116)	7 (54)	6 (42)	4 (28)	3 (20)	2 (15)
Spain	34 (79)	17 (30)	9 (20)	4 (15)	2 (9)	- (6)
Austria	11 (54)	3 (25)	2 (14)	2 (10)	2 (7)	1 (4)
Finland	7 (52)	1 (29)	1 (20)	1 (17)	- (12)	- (9)
Portugal	6 (10)	1 (3)	- (2)	- (0)	- (0)	- (9)
Total	3,502 (10,373)	1,948 (5,586)	1,371 (4,027)	1,060 (3,124)	852 (2,494)	648 (2,050)

Source: Adapted from Tables 1 and 3 in U.N. ECOSOC Document E/C. 10/58 23 March 1979.

7

TABLE 1.2. Firms with one or more foreign affiliates, by developing host region, 1977

Number of firms with foreign affiliates in developing countries

Firms based in:	Total	Western Hemisphere only	Asia only	Africa only	More than one of the three regions	In each of the three regions
United States of America	1,197	522	130	53	492	166
United Kingdom	639	97	176	102	264	136
Germany, Federal Republic of	316	134	57	29	96	20
Switzerland	109	48	11	6	44	12
Netherlands	104	28	18	10	48	21
France	246	36	19	125	66	27
Canada	121	77	12	9	23	11
Japan	225	46	77	5	97	20
Belgium	90	16	2	49	23	8
Australia	181	11	150	1	19	2
Italy	58	23	7	9	19	7
Sweden	63	27	5	3	28	10
New Zealand	58	2	55	-	1	-
Denmark	22	7	4	4	7	2
Norway	15	4	5	-	6	3
Spain	34	22	3	4	5	-
Austria	11	3	5	1	2	1
Finland	7	4	-	2	1	-
Portugal	6	2	1	3	-	-
Total	3,502	1,109	737	415	1,241	446

Source: Adapted from Table 4 in U.N. ECOSOC Document E/C. 10/58, 23 March 1979.

TABLE 1.3. Distribution of firms based in developed market economies, by size (Percentage)

	Sales of more than $1 billion	Sales of more than $395 million	Firms with most employees
United States of America	54.2	49.2	48.5
Japan	11.9	13.3	3.5
United Kingdom	10.0	9.7	18.8
Germany, Federal Republic of	6.6	6.8	8.1
France	4.9	4.8	7.3
Sweden	2.4	2.9	3.1
Canada	2.2	3.5	1.5
Switzerland	1.7	1.6	1.9
Spain	1.2	1.3	-
Italy	1.0	1.3	3.1
Netherlands	1.0	1.0	2.3
Belgium	0.7	0.8	0.8
Total a/	100.0	100.0	100.0
Number	411	872	260

Source: See tables 1 and 5; Commission of the European Communities, Survey of Multinational Enterprises (Brussels, 1976), vol.
1, pp. 50-51, table H; Fortune, May and August 1977.

the astonishing power attained by Japan through its multinational operations, despite the fact that Japanese firms have gone "multinational" extensively only since the late 1960s.

While from table 1.1 it is evident that MNC parent headquarters are concentrated in the industrialized countries of the world, it should be noted that a few large firms, mostly Western-controlled, have established corporate headquarters in Latin America and Africa. Indeed, of the 500 largest MNCs in the world, 34 are now headquartered in LDCs.

Geographic location as well as the economic sector are important determinants for the size of affiliates. The average size of affiliates in developing countries is only half that in developed countries, partly because the affiliates serve only local markets (especially when it comes to import-substituting industries), while in developed countries they serve large national or regional markets as in the case of the European Community. (19) In terms of economic sector, affiliates in the extractive industries are usually three to four times larger than in manufacturing sectors.

The global linkages created by MNCs are also reflected in the foreign investment patterns. United States direct investment has continued to climb in developing countries from 1970 to 1977, but outflows to manufacturing affiliates have declined for the last three consecutive years. (20) However, investment in the petroleum sector, after manifesting a nose dive in 1974, has reversed itself and large investments in this sector have been made in Latin America. Capital expenditures by majority-owned foreign affiliates of United States companies in the Third World dipped during 1975 and 1976, but have resumed their upward movement since then (see fig. 1.1). Of course, data vary greatly from country to country. (21) In this connection, it must be kept in mind that MNCs continue to do most of their business in the developed countries, and that United States direct foreign investment during the 1970s was four times as large in the latter countries than in the Third World. But the establishment of new subsidiaries by the major American MNCs has been dropping sharply in both developed and Third World countries, (22) a trend that appears to continue and is reinforced by the declining value of the United States dollar.

Looking at the global investment picture, table 1.4 shows that in terms of investment by sector, the general thrust in developing countries has been in favor of the extractive industries in all regions except Latin America and the Caribbean. Table 1.5 provides data on direct investments in the developing world by major OECD countries, and table 1.6 depicts the distribution of new investments and reinvestments of some of these countries. It is interesting to note that while United States investments have declined sharply from 1975 to 1976, those of Japan, Canada, and Belgium have risen. (23) Overall investments in the Third World by major OECD countries, which had risen from $2.5 billion to $10.5 billion during the 1965-75 decade, also declined sharply to $7.6 billion. (24) Interestingly, as fig. 1.2 shows, Brazil, Mexico, India, Malaysia, and the tax havens increased their share of foreign investments appreciably, while that of other LDCs including OPEC (1975) declined.

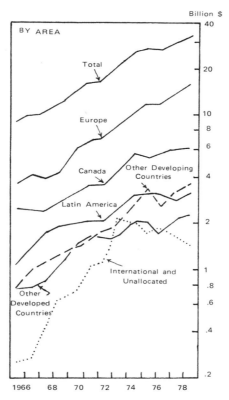

Fig. 1.1.   Capital Expenditure by Majority-owned Foreign
Affiliates of United States Companies.

Source: Department of Commerce, <u>Survey of Current Business</u> 58,
no. 3 (March 1978):   25.

Unequal Capabilities and Dependence

The basic reason that under certain circumstances interdependence
conjures up fears of dependence on the part of governments or private
sectors is the inequality of capabilities within the interdependence
relationship. Instead of producing perceptions of <u>reciprocal</u> dependence
that might induce governments to treat the acts of other governments
or of private entities such as MNCs as though they were events within
their own borders and might be seen within the context of converging, if
not identical, interests, <u>unequal</u> capabilities among states are likely to
lead to suspicion, envy, and tensions. Hence, governmental leaders may
feel called upon to resort to national means and solutions as a
countervailing force against the real or imagined threat of dependence
on international business and other countries. Such actions harm the
prospects of useful collaboration among states and are likely to
undermine, if not destroy, the benefits which transnational business

TABLE 1.4. Stock of Direct Investment in Developing Host Countries, by Region and Industrial Sector, End 1972

Region	Petroleum	Mining and Smelting	Manufac- turing	Other	Total all sectors	Share of total
		(Billions of dollars)				(Percentage)
Africa	4.1	1.5	1.6	1.9	9.1	20.7
Latin America and Caribbean	5.3	2.2	8.9	6.2	22.6	51.5
Middle East	3.6	-	0.3	0.2	4.1	9.3
Asia and Oceana	2.4	0.6	2.5	2.6	8.1	18.4
Total, all regions	15.4	4.3	13.3	10.9	43.9	100.0
Percentage of total	35.0	9.8	30.3	24.8	100.0	

Source: United Nations Center on Transnational Corporations, based on data from the Organization for Economic Cooperation and Development.

TABLE 1.5. Distribution of Direct Investment Flows from OECD Member Countries(a) to Developing Countries by Country of Origin - 1965-1976

(Percentage Share)

Country	Annual Average 1965-1967	1970-1972	1973	1974	1975	1976
United States	51.1	49.2	43.0	53.5	69.0	41.1
Japan	3.6	5.9	19.4	10.0	2.1	14.3
Germany, Federal Republic of	6.5	11.0	11.7	9.9	7.8	10.1
United Kingdom	9.1	8.3	10.4	10.1	7.6	9.5
Canada	1.5	2.7	1.9	2.7	2.8	5.7
France	15.1	5.5	4.3	3.4	2.6	3.2
Netherlands	4.0	5.4	1.3	3.4	2.2	3.2
Belgium	2.1	1.1	0.7	0.7	0.7	3.1
Switzerland	2.1	1.7	1.2	1.8	2.0	3.0
Italy	2.6	5.3	3.7	1.4	1.4	2.8
Sweden	1.2	1.0	0.3	0.7	0.8	1.6
Australia	1.0	2.2	1.6	1.7	0.5	1.0
Other countries(b)	0.2	0.9	0.5	0.7	0.5	1.4
Grand Total	100.0	100.0	100.0	100.0	100.0	100.0

(a) Countries are listed in descending order of percentage share for 1976.
(b) Austria, Denmark, New Zealand, Norway, Finland; figures prior to 1972 exclude Finland and New Zealand.

Source: United Nations, Center on Transnational Corporations, based on OECD, Development Cooperation (Paris, issues fo 1974 to 1977).

TABLE 1.6. Direct Investment Flow from Selected Developed Marked Economies to Developing Countries by Type of Flow - 1965-1976 (millions of dollars)

Country and Type of Flow	1965-67	1970-72	Annual Average 1973	1974	1975	1976
Australia:						
Total	22	85	104	117	48	75
New Investment	22	67	26	28	43	44
Reinvested earnings	-	18	78	89	5	31
Belgium:						
Total	47	44	48	49	69	236
New Investment	7	27	22	23	43	215
Reinvested Earnings	40	17	26	26	26	20
Canada:						
Total	34	105	125	193	300	430
New Investment	25	39	50	109	150	205
Reinvested Earnings	9	66	75	84	150	225
Germany, Federal Republic of:						
Total	147	426	787	701	816	765
New Investment	84	265	543	431	532	487
Reinvested Earnings	63	161	244	270	284	278
Italy:						
Total	59	206	246	100	150	213
New Investment	44	137	136	-15	40	83
Reinvested Earnings	15	69	110	115	110	130
Sweden:						
Total	27	39	22	49	82	125
New Investment	19	31	12	29	57	116
Reinvested Earnings	8	8	10	20	26	9
United States:						
Total	1,147	1,909	2,887	3,788	7,241	3,119
New Investment	771	1,287	1,675	2,035	4,010	1,850
Reinvested Earnings	376	622	1,212	1,753	3,231	1.269
Total above countries:						
Total	1,483	2,814	4,219	4,997	8,705	4,963
New Investment	972	1,855	2,464	2,640	4,875	3,000
Reinvested Earnings	511	961	1,755	2,357	3,830	1,963

Source: United Nations, Center on Transnational Corporations, based on OECD, Development Cooperation (Paris, issues for 1974 to 1977).

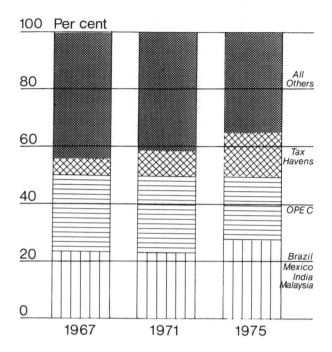

NOTE: OPEC countries include Algeria, Ecuador, Gabon, Indonesia, Iran, Iraq, Kuwait, Libyan Arab Jamahiriya, Nigeria, Qatar, Saudi Arabia, United Arab Emirates and Venezuela. Tax havens include Bahamas, Barbados, Bermuda, Cayman Islands, Netherlands Antilles, and Panama.

Fig. 1.2. Foreign direct investment stock in developing countries, 1967-1975.

Source: CTC Reporter 1, no. 4 (April 1978): 5.

networks may produce for the transfer of ideas, technology, know-how, and capital. Perceptions of this dependence (25) have aggravated all the other problems that many leaders of the developing countries have faced in their priority task of nation-building and their consequent preoccupation with sovereignty and autonomy of choice.

While these leaders may perceive various degrees of dependence and restrictions on their autonomy flowing from MNC operations in their countries, there is also a reverse dependence on certain developing countries on the part of most developed countries and many of the MNCs headquartered there. This dependence relationship stems from the need for certain raw materials, especially petroleum and a number of nonfuel strategic raw materials such as bauxite, manganese, tungsten, zinc, and others. However, the interdependence pattern that emerges for the relationship between MNCs, industrial countries, and Third World states reflects a high degree of asymmetry. In terms of MNC investments and the number of links between parent companies and affiliates, the density of the network is about twice as great among industrialized nations as between MNC units located in advanced and developing countries. Moreover, as we have seen, the number of MNC affiliates in the Third World varies considerably from country to country and by industrial sector. As for minerals to feed the industrial machinery of the advanced countries, we observe selective mineral dependence of a substantial magnitude. Since MNC operations are heavily involved in the North-South transactional flows by providing significant capabilities for the satisfaction of needs across national boundaries - both for the advanced and developing countries - they make MNCs active and crucial participants in the minerals aspect of the interdependence web. In carrying out their functions, they may be seen as angels or devils, depending on where the observer sits. The interdependence problem is compounded by the politically sensitive fact that outside their home countries MNCs earn 25 percent of the GNP of the noncommunist world with United States-based operations producing abroad five times what they export from the United States. (26)

As already noted, during recent years, United States foreign policy has regarded growing interdependence as not only inevitable, but also desirable in producing consensus and restraining unacceptable conduct by foreign governments. It is viewed as a positive value in the expanding relationship between advanced and developing countries, and MNCs are considered as playing a beneficial role by their capabilities of bringing technology, skills, goods, and services to LDCs. Indeed, the State Department has promoted the notion of purposefully pursuing a strategy of interdependence, (27) and that includes the deliberate support of larger entities such as the European Community and Comecon. In United States-Soviet relations, interdependence is pursued as a pragmatic mechanism by both sides as an alternative to unwanted confrontation and unattainable friendship, and in response to a perceived political imperative.

Secretary of State Kissinger articulated this strategy necessity in a speech in Boston on March 11, 1976:

...The interdependence of nations - the indivisibility of our security and our prosperity - can accelerate our common progress or our common decline.

Therefore, just as we must seek to move beyond a balance of power in East-West relations, so must we transcend tests of strength in North-South relations and build a true world community.

We do so in our self-interest, for today's web of economic relationships links the destinies of all mankind. The price and supply of energy, the conditions of trade, the expansion of world food production, the technological bases for economic development, the protection of the world's environment, the rules of law governing the world's oceans and outer space -- these are concerns that affect all nations and can be satisfactorily addressed only in a framework of international cooperation. (28)

However, the views of the former Secretary are not shared in all quarters.   Many Third World representatives as well as a number of Western intellectuals look at interdependence as creating undesirable dependence, and some think it is a code word for economic bondage. (29)   They see a widening gap between affluent and poor societies and do not consider that the masses in the Third World benefit from MNC operations.   For these observers, the process of interdependence escalates tensions over the restrictions of national or societal autonomy, threatens the achievement of national economic, social, and political objectives, and may produce violent nationalist and interstate conflict.

THIRD WORLD STRATEGIES AGAINST DEPENDENCY

Deep apprehension about their countries' dependence on the industrialized states in general and on MNCs in particular, as well as the possible opportunities that might flow from certain asymmetries in economic interdependence relationships, has led Third World leaders to use various United Nations forums to develop strategies and initiate attacks against the perceived encroachment from current and prospective MNC activities on their governmental autonomy.

When, in the 1950s and 1960s, most of the former colonial countries received their independence, many of their leaders anticipated that international and regional development efforts would bring substantial improvements in their economic status.   In 1961, the first United Nations Development Decade was launched with great fanfare.   The European Economic Community (EEC) expanded its association program in Africa with the first Yaounde Convention of 1963.   In Latin America, the Alliance of Progress was initiated in 1961 with the expectation that the level of economic development could be raised substantially in ten years.   However, these initiatives did not produce the hoped-for economic results, although the Yaounde Convention fared better than the regional effort in Latin America.   At the same time, the leadership in the Third World began to realize that while achieving political independence did, indeed, provide formal equality with other countries, many facets of dependence on the former masters remained in economic and administrative areas, materially reducing their freedom of choice.

A major forum for efforts to improve the economic ills of the Third World was, and remains, the United Nations Conference on Trade and Development (UNCTAD) established in 1963 and holding its first meeting in 1964 in Geneva, Switzerland.   UNCTAD was organized mainly by a group of 77 developing countries which became known as the Group of "77", although by now it comprises nearly 120 states. Through UNCTAD, the Third World attempted to achieve several major objectives: industrialization, the elimination of tariff barriers for goods manufactured in the developing countries and imported into the developed countries, the stabilization of prices for primary commodities exported from Third World countries and the financing of such a scheme by the industrially advanced states, reduction or elimination of debts owed by the Third World, and outright development assistance grants pegged at first to 1 percent of GNP of the developed countries and later, more realistically, lowered to 0.7 percent.

In connection with these objectives, the impact MNCs might have on the process of development prompted the initiation of various studies in different United Nations bodies in the late 1960s. These studies, in turn, resulted in a number of reports and resolutions. As early as 1968, the Sixth Asian Regional Conference of the International Labour Organization (ILO) urged the ILO Governing Body to address itself to the question of management-labor relations, including those of MNCs. At the Ninth Conference of American States Members of ILO, questions were raised regarding the effects of MNC policies on working and living conditions in countries where MNCs operate. Finally, in 1971, the Governing Body of the ILO undertook to assess the relationship between MNCs and social policy. (30)

UNCTAD also passed a number of resolutions in 1972 dealing with the relationship of foreign private investment to development, to restrictive business practices (especially of MNCs), and to the transfer of technology. These resolutions had their origin in studies made by the UNCTAD Secretariat and they proposed a variety of actions, including the establishment of ad hoc groups of experts to come up with solutions reflecting Third World interests. (31)

Perhaps the most significant resolution on the subject of MNCs was passed in July 1972 by the United Nations Economic and Social Council (ECOSOC) (no. 161-LIII). (32) Adopted unanimously, it formally and explicitly recognized the importance of MNCs as a subject for comprehensive study and possible action by the United Nations organization. This resolution refers to the ILO and UNCTAD efforts regarding MNCs, and has become the major trigger for subsequent actions taken by the United Nations Secretary General and for the initiation of negotiations on a code of conduct for MNCs.

The multiple attack through the United Nations on what Third World governments perceived to be adverse effects of MNC operations in their countries was complemented by the endeavors to introduce a new international economic order (NIEO). Within the framework of the Second United Nations Development Decade, the General Assembly, in December 1972, passed Resolution 3016 (XXVII) affirming the permanent sovereignty of the developing states over their natural resources. This was reiterated by the United Nations Economic and Social Council through a similar resolution in May 1973. (33) In May 1974, the General Assembly adopted the Declaration on the Establishment of a New International Economic Order plus a Programme of Action for implementation (Resolutions 3201 and 3202 [S-VI]), which offered a comprehensive plan revamping traditional relations and interactions and, thereby, affecting MNC practices and activities. The Charter of Economic Rights and Duties of States (Resolution 321 [XXIX]), adopted in December 1974, also contains clauses that have a bearing on MNCs, especially as far as natural resources and expropriations are concerned. Finally, the General Assembly resolutions of September 1975 regarding Development and International Economic Co-operation (3362 [S-VII]) affects MNCs with respect to technology transfer and the establishment of new manufacturing subsidiaries. (34)

The NIEO has been called a political offensive and it is within the political, rather than economic, context that has been created by the adoption of the various United Nations resolutions on North-South issues mentioned above, that the search for MNC codes of conduct has been proceeding. This will become quite obvious as we examine the drawn-out, often acrimonious negotiations within the United Nations' structures on the subject. The next chapter will discuss the origins of these negotiations.

2 Problem Areas of MNCs in Third World Countries

Although investment in the Third World is less than one-third of total direct foreign investment by MNCs, the problems and questions arising from MNC activities in LDCs are both much more intensive and broader than those encountered in advanced countries. Two main reasons account for this disparity: (a) the differences in scale between the operations of huge MNCs and the relatively small size and primitive nature of many LDC economies; and (b) the often extraordinary difference in power between MNC home and host governments. The problems are compounded by two peripheral, though very significant, issues: the achievement of economic growth and development in the Third World, and the changing perceptions about the value of private enterprise. It is by considering these two persepctives that MNC problem areas in the Third World such as balance of payments, trade, employment, taxation, transfer of technology and skills, and political, social, and cultural effects of MNC activities need to be evaluated. A large body of so-called MNC impact literature has accumulated during the last decade, attesting to the very topical nature of our problem area.

A major question in the MNC-LDC relationships is the distribution of benefits and drawbacks for the parties involved, and since perceptions regarding these factors depend very much on where participants or observers "sit," (1) much disagreement exists as to what is a benefit or drawback for whom. Of course, where you sit also influences your behavior and, therefore, conflict has crept into many of the MNC-Third World relationships.

BALANCE-OF-PAYMENTS PROBLEMS

In most Third World countries except the oil producers, the balance-of-payment situation is precarious. Imports of manufactured goods are

20

often high and servicing extensive loans made to LDCs by industrialized countries and multilateral financial institutions imposes a heavy burden. Therefore, inflows of investment capital ($7.6 billion in 1976 from the OECD countries) provide distinct benefits to the balance of payments of the Third World, but earnings generated by past investments and then repatriated change the picture drastically. Between 1965 and 1970, a sample of 43 developing countries showed that net inflow of foreign direct investment was 68 percent of outflow not considering oil producing countries, and if these countries had been included it would have reduced the inflow to 30 percent of outflow. (2) This deficit has been a source of tension between MNC subsidiary managements and LDC governments, especially when local MNC operations have been carried on for several years without inflow of new capital. The tension is heightened when parent-company governments compel repatriation of profits either by executive action or by enactment of special laws or impede outflow of funds. This was the case when in 1968 the United States government introduced control measures in the flow of capital and the return of profits. However, we should note that United States provisions were much less stringent for investments and reinvestment earnings in LDCs than in advanced countries. (3)

There is another side to the balance-of-payments coin that more often than not benefits the LDC host countries. MNC affiliates engage in exports and imports which would not, in many cases, be undertaken by local business. Many manufacturing subsidiaries of MNCs produce goods that go beyond import substitution and channel their products to established markets in third countries. Thus they add to export totals of LDCs and may reduce net imports, although manufacturing plants may require materials and supplies that also have to be brought in. Of course, extractive industries are the most substantial exporters, but the materials exported are the resources of the host country, and some LDC governments regard past and present MNC activities in these industries as "exploitation" and, therefore, exports of the resources are often not seen as MNC-related "benefits." But MNCs have also contributed significantly to the exports of finished goods such as automobile parts which in Latin America has been developed from several countries, Brazil (4) in particular. If indeed all the MNC-generated exports are counted, the effects on the balance of payments in the Third World are positive - for example, in Latin America in 1966 United States affiliates exported about $4.5 billion of their products and imported $1.3 billion of materials and supplies. (5)

There are other factors that have impacts on the balance-of-payments of an LDC. Examples are export restrictions set by the MNCs to suit their own objectives or tied purchases. (6) Such activities may reduce undesirable competition among the affiliates, but at the same time they damage the prospects of the host country for the expansion of exports from its territory. Perhaps the most important factor is overpricing of goods imported from an MNC affiliate outside the host country and underpricing of products manufactured in the host country by the affiliate when exported to a third affiliate abroad. This raises one of the thorniest problems in MNC-LDC relations, which is transfer pricing. Since its impact goes beyond affecting balance of payments, we will return to it later.

In addition to the direct impact of MNC operations on the balance of payments of host countries, some indirect effects must be mentioned. The establishment of MNC affiliates in LDCs raises income and, thereby, may increase the consumption of imports and reduce the supply of locally manufactured goods for exports. On the other hand, the affiliates may stimulate the creation of complementary industries that, in turn, might produce additional goods for exports. Thus, the indirect effects of new MNC affiliates and existing MNC operations on the balance-of-payments situation depends on the particular circumstances in individual LDCs and, in some cases, may be positive or negative. (7)

THE MNC IMPACT ON EMPLOYMENT

Developing countries with large-scale unemployment and relatively well-educated populations have benefited from the establishment of MNC affiliates which used low-cost labor for the manufacture of parts for electronics and other high-technology products to be sold in established markets, mainly in the advanced countries of the world. Taiwan, South Korea, and Singapore are some of the countries that have benefited from such investments and where, as a consequence, the economic levels of their people as a whole have risen. Other developing countries, such as Mauritius, have geared their current development plans to attracting appropriate MNCs for similar purposes. In 1972 an American MNC opened a small assembling subsidiary in Mauritius and advertised the availability of 50 trainee positions paying 36 cents a day. More than 1,000 individuals applied who, in their anxiety to obtain a job, broke all the windows of the employment office. However, in overall terms, employment by MNC subsidiaries in the Third World remains relatively low. Although definite figures are difficult to obtain, some observers put the total number at three to four million in 1976, while others estimate it only at two million.

In addition to increased employment, the establishment of MNC affiliates in LDCs has other effects. New skills are taught that may be useful for local entrepreneurs and the wages paid by MNC affiliates are normally higher than those prevailing in the country. Additional employment sources may be created through the increased use of local suppliers and ancillary services.

It is precisely these effects, seen as major benefits by some observers, that are criticized as intolerable drawbacks by others. The critics claim that MNC affiliates often import technologies that are mostly capital-intensive with minimum labor requirements and thus disregard the pervasive unemployment (30 percent of total labor force) and underemployment that plague the Third World. (8) Moreover, higher wages paid by MNC affiliates may lead to demands by employees of local firms for similar increases. This may create severe competition, especially for technical personnel, and cause difficulties for local companies. At the same time, the higher wages may fuel inflationary pressures and, equally bad, reduce the competitiveness of local businesses because of their low operational efficiency. As MNC affiliates continue to operate in a particular host country, disparities are likely to deepen the already existing economic and social gap between rural and urban areas with the poorest part of the rural population often seeing no improvement in income at all. Such developments cannot help but generate frictions and may make the establishment of MNC affiliates unwelcome in some of the LDCs.

Another source of tension is the impact on local labor when MNCs decide to close plants in LDCs in accordance with global corporate designs. While this may not happen frequently, it is an event that will be published widely and create adversity for all MNC investment initiatives and operations.

Finally, organized labor plays a role in these situations. While the increased wages paid MNC affiliates provide incentives for existing labor organizations to level up wages generally, the emerging disparities in wages may induce governmental leaders to oppose such endeavors. Moreover, national business firms, already at a competitive disadvantage because of the higher efficiency of MNC affiliates, may pressure the government to halt efforts at leveling up wages. Another dimension and source of friction may be governmental concern in LDCs that if wages are driven up too far, MNC affiliates may close their plants. As a consequence, some of the governmental decision makers in the developing world have passed legislation either forbidding strikes in general or prohibiting strikes against American corporations, as was done in Korea. In Singapore, labor legislation has also been enacted recently which is designed to keep union activity and wages down. It is not inconceivable that other developing countries, which have begun to benefit from the influx of industry into their territories, may follow the example of Singapore in order to protect the benefits they are now receiving in terms of higher employment. Since, on the other hand, some of the union activities aim at influencing the legislative process in the developing countries to obtain favorable laws for organizing workers and protecting their rights, tension arises in these countries. In some cases, labor laws have been enacted which give lip service to the freedom of action by trade unions and are vague with respect to collective bargaining. At the same time, govermental control remains pervasive and unions are used for the mobilization of support for the government.

The governmental elites in some LDCs are often fearful that unions, if successful in their aims, will create new positions of power competing with those that the new leadership in the developing countries has recently established. (9) This is likely to induce the governmental elites to fall back on rekindling the fires of nationalism and branding the activities of international labor as a disturbing foreign element for the development of the newly independent countries. Although the technical assistance furnished by certain of the international unions is clearly beneficial to workers in some LDCs, the national governments may seek to downgrade these efforts in order to prevent the local population from forming a favorable image of foreign unions. (10) Indeed, strong labor movements exist only in Argentina and Honduras, while in many other Third World countries labor unions are fledgling organizations (11) struggling to obtain recognition by the national governments for the pursuit of their usual task to organize employees for collective bargaining.

The governmental leaders in developing countries may also seek alliances with national businessmen who are concerned that the higher wages paid by foreign employers will disrupt their traditional mode of doing business. National employers may give aid to the interests of the political leadership by stimulating frictions between the labor employed by themselves and the workers of foreign companies. Thus, national employers together with their workers (and local trade unions where they exist) could become allies of the indigenous political leadership in a nationalist opposition to foreign or multinational business and foreign trade union penetration.

THE TRANSFER OF TECHNOLOGY

Technology can be transferred by licensing agreements or through the medium of the MNC either by the use of existing multinational facilities or investment in a new facility in a foreign country. Licensing agreements, which do not require any border-crossing capital or foreign ownership of industrial installations, have been successful vehicles for large numbers of patent and technological know-how transfers. In many cases, independent national private firms are involved and, in some instances, these agreements have led to transnational business collaboration arrangements between two companies of different nationalities encompassing joint production and marketing activities.

It is noteworthy that in 1970 developing countries held only 6 percent of all the patents issued throughout the world and that 80 percent of these patents granted in the Third World went to firms located in five countries (the United States, West Germany, Switzerland, the United Kingdom, and France). In fact, nationals of developing countries hold less than 1 percent of the world total of patents. (12)

Despite the apparent need for technology on the part of Third World countries, more than 90 percent of all technology transfers take place between industrialized countries. Moreover, about two-thirds of the licensing arrangements are found in the industrial countries of Europe, Canada, and Australia. In Latin America and Asia these agreements are relatively new, but constitute a growing method of transnational business. In Africa, they are concentrated in the Republic of South Africa. Generally, in the Third World the agreements require more assistance with plant facilities, machinery, and marketing than potential licensors are prepared to offer. At the same time, fewer potential licensees limit the opportunities. (13) Regardless of how many licenses or patents are bought, the cost is high. Taken as a group, developing countries have paid about $1.1 billion in 1975 to the developed countries for licenses, patents, trademarks, etc. Over half of these payments were made by Latin American states, particularly the larger, more advanced countries such as Mexico and Brazil. These payments continue to grow and absorb an increasing portion of LDC export earnings. (For data regarding seven LDCs, see table 2.1.) It has been estimated that by 1985 LDCs will payover $6 billion for technology if the current rates of growth are maintained. (14)

Since some technical knowledge is not offered under licenses without substantial equity ownership (especially United States companies are becoming increasingly reluctant to part with technology without such a safeguard), (15) facilities of MNCs in host countries have become the means for the inflow of new technologies. In some instances, formal licensing arrangements have also been made within multinational corporate structures, but whether such agreements are legally acceptable is a matter of dispute. (16) In any case, such agreements could restrict the flow of know-how that otherwise should become available from the parent company's pool of knowledge and expertise: research skills, production techniques, and management capability. It is precisely this combination that can make transfer of technology through the structures of the MNC so important. A possible additional advantage of such knowledge transmission is that the parent company may charge its subsidiary less than the market price for the knowledge it transmits, resulting either in lower prices for the host country consumer or higher profits for the subsidiary.

A midway house for the transfer of technology between the fully owned affiliate of an MNC and licensing agreements is the joint equity venture formed by a multinational corporation and a host country company. While under this arrangement the involvement of MNC management is reduced, there is likely to be a better appreciation of local economic conditions and needs, thereby enhancing the relations with the host government.

The contribution of technology and management skills to the operations of MNC affiliates abroad made by the parent organization often spreads beyond the confines of the affiliates in host countries. As Jack N. Behrman points out, commercial activities tend to spread managerial and technical contributions to customers and suppliers of the affiliates. Customers are provided with products of higher quality, perhaps at lower cost and better adapted to local conditions. Technical services include counseling the customer on his product needs and on ways of increasing his productivity. At the same time, MNC affiliates can assist suppliers in the construction of their plants and equipment layouts, thereby helping in the production of a higher quality of goods for use by the affiliate and other users, in a particular foreign country. (17)

An important question regarding the transfer of technology is its

TABLE 2.1. Payment of Royalties and Fees by Selected Developing Countries, Latest Available Year

| | | Payments of Royalties and Fees | |
Country	Year	Millions of Dollars	Percentage of Exports
Argentina	1974	101	2.56
Brazil	1976	272	2.68
Chile	1972	17	1.98
Colombia	1975	17	1.16
Mexico	1971	167	11.11
Trinidad and Tobago	1975	18	1.02
India*	1973	24	0.81

*Fiscal year ending 31 March.

Source: United Nations, Center on Transnational Corporations, based on Argentina: International Monetary Fund, Balance of Payments Yearbook, vol. 27; Brazil: Banco Central de Brazil, Annual Report, 1976, April 1977; Chile: Banco Central de Chile, Balanza de Pagos, 1972; Colombia: Banco de la Republica, Informe anual del Gerente a la Junta Directiva, 1975; Mexico: F. Fajnzylber and T.M. Tanago, "Las empresas transnacionales, expansion a nivel mundial y projeccion en la industria mexicana," (Mexico, Fondo de Cultural Economica, 1976); Trinidad and Tobago: Central Statistical Office, The Balance of Payments of Trinidad and Tobago, 1975; India: Indian Investment Center, India, A Profile of Progress, January 1976.

appropriateness for LDCs. We have already mentioned the extensive unemployment and underemployment in many of these countries and, therefore, the importation of capital-intensive technology may not only be irrelevant but, indeed, harmful to the solution of Third World problems. (18)

Whatever benefits Third World host country governments may expect to derive from the transfer of technologies, they may also be apprehensive that in the case of serious needs such transfers may be withheld either by decision of the headquarters company or by the government of the country in which that company or the parent company is located. The United States, the major "exporter" of technology in the world, has two principal laws on its books, The Trading with the Enemy Act of 1917 and the Export Control Act of 1949, under which the government can deny another country access to goods or technology generated by affiliates more than 50 percent United States owned in that country or a third country. Moreover, multinational corporations pursuing their own self-interests may use the transfer of technology to bargain for more favorable and flexible treatment. Thus, the ability of MNCs to transfer technology to the host countries of its affiliates creates serious dilemmas for the governmental decision makers and conjures up vistas of intolerable dependence. Governments fear that without national sources of technological advance, their economic development will be impeded and their military and political influence reduced. To advance technology independently requires facilities for fundamental research within the national boundaries that are frequently beyond the financial capabilities of domestic firms and even governments.

In attempting to solve the dilemma, governments can choose from the following options:

1. Forego the acquisition of certain advanced technologies such as space exploration that in fact may not contribute to their particular needs.

2. Generate the necessary funds for setting up domestically owned facilities for the development of needed technologies.

3. Import technology by purchase of the desired products.

4. Import technology by permitting the establishment of foreign-owned production facilities for the desired items. (19)

For most governments, especially in the Third World, the cost of purchasing technological independence is excessive, and they must lean toward options one and four. The latter option provides some control over the MNC affiliate that is the vehicle for importing the technology because it is located within the borders of the host country. At the same time, host governments seek to reduce dependence by urging MNCs to establish local research and development facilities. The extent to which this request is followed varies greatly. Some have established separate R&D institutes, while others have authorized affiliates to create appropriate research and development sections.

However, the bulk of research efforts is generally concentrated in the parent organization or is directly under its control, although affiliates are frequently encouraged to perform development work for the local market or for improving locally used processes. Thus, dependence of host governments may not be eliminated, but somewhat alleviated, by such practices.

However, even if relatively independent R&D institutes or affiliate sections are established in host countries, additional drawbacks may have to be considered. These institutes may stifle the creation of domestically owned research bases, and they may adversely affect the local supply of scientific and engineering talent to locally owned R&D organizations. In fact, MNC affiliates are known to have purchased fully manned and equipped research institutes from domestic owners.

These considerations suggest that despite the substantial benefits host countries can derive from technological transfers, they are also sources of tensions, stimulate perceptions of threats by the MNC in the minds of host governments and other elites, and carry with them some objective drawbacks as well. This situation is aggravated in the Third World where (rightly or wrongly) industrialization looms large as the most effective means for economic development, but where, at the same time, resentment has grown about the high cost, both in monetary and dependency terms, of necessary technology for the industrialization process. Some observers have claimed that not only will indigeneous inventive activity be discouraged, but local entrepreneurship may be suppressed as well. (20)

What can host governments do to counter the possibility that foreign and especially United States-owned affiliates of MNCs become tools for the foreign policy implementation toward a third country through restrictions of technology transfers? One preventive step is refusal to authorize the establishment of an MNC affiliate or to insist that majority ownership is in the hands of its own citizens or of a public corporation. Another method is passage of a law which compels MNC affiliates to carry out directives and policies within carefully spelled-out areas, regardless of ownership considerations. A final, very drastic measure would be the threat of expropriation, which may, however, be blunted by the fear of retaliation when industrially advanced countries among which extensive MNC ties exist are involved.

TRANSFER PRICING AND TAXES

One of the factors having aroused the greatest apprehension of Third World countries about MNC affiliates operating within their territories has been the intracompany "transfer-pricing." In order to raise global profits, prices on intracompany transfers of goods produced in different countries or on the fees set for technology (licenses, patents, or costs of knowledge) charged to affiliates across national boundaries are set artificially in such a way as to take advantage of the lowest taxes in the countries involved and the most favorable currency exchange rates. Profits can be enhanced further by the purposeful search for low-tax countries in which to establish production and assembly facilities. In some cases, underpriced products may be shipped to a tax-haven country such as the Bahamas and re-exported with highly inflated prices to a third country for final sale. The result is that the country in which these goods are manufactured loses tax revenues that it would have received if transactions had been carried out between independent buyers and sellers, so-called arm's length transactions.

Barnet and Muller cite studies made on the overpricing of imports through MNC channels in several industries in Latin America. According to these studies, the following average overpricing took place in Colombia: 155 percent by the pharmaceutical firms, 16 to 60 percent by the electronic industry, and 40 percent by the rubber firms. In Peru, overpricing ranged from 75 to 300 percent, and in Ecuador, 75 to 200 percent in various industries. (21)

Tax avoidance through manipulating import and export prices is only one way that MNCs benefit from having affiliates in different countries. In the event that host countries place limitations on the repatriation of profits, astute transfer pricing may help avoid leaving too many earnings in those countries. Moreover, the reporting of low profits in a particular country might be an excellent public-image strategy to fend off attacks of "exploitation." On the other hand, overpricing of imports may harm the economy and social welfare of the recipient LDC by making, for example, the cost of essential drugs prohibitive for much of the population and impeding economic development by driving up the cost of key industrial installations and important consumer goods.

MNCs AND HOST COUNTRY POLICIES

It has been argued that the more responsibility for economic growth the government accepts, the greater its control over the economy, and the greater the possibility that the MNC will be viewed as a potential disturber of economic plans. (22)

Although MNCs and their affiliates can make substantial contributions to the economic growth of host countries, they can also inject uncertainties into the economies of these countries by altering economic factors and reducing the government's ability to predict reactions to its plans, in that MNCs may be able to ignore government persuasions and pursue policies not supportive of the national goals. In particular, they may cause uncertainties and risks by creating economic disequilibria through concentration of foreign ownership in key industries, overinvestment in equipment industries resulting in over-capacities, producing deficits in the balance of payments, and causing disturbances in the labor market. These MNC capabilities flow, at least in part, from options available to management regarding the direction of future investments and the use of various sources of funds. Having alternative investment opportunities elsewhere in the world, MNC managements may not respond to the incentives that would be sufficient for a decision desired by the government of a domestically owned firm. Moreover, the ability to shift funds among the components of an MNC through intracompany sales, technical assistance fees, royalties, and allocation of headquarters expenses may have impacts on the host country's balance of payments that may be harmful to host government goals. In addition, these shifts in funds reinforce already existing currency-exchange pressures; in fact, threatening disturbances in the exchange market may have caused the fund movements in the first place because corporation treasurers wanted to safeguard or even improve their overall assets when devaluations or revaluations of national currencies appeared to be likely.

The disturbance of governmental objectives and policies is perceived as especially serious by LDC leaders because they continue to be faced with the needs of nation-building within an environment of poverty, illiteracy, and traditional political cultures. Overarching is their natural desire to retain their positions of political power. Suspicion and distrust of MNC operations in LDCs is deepened further by the experiences and backgrounds of many Third World governmental leaders and political elites. Most of them have experienced the trauma of colonialism, which instilled in them a fear of foreign capital as something inherently evil because it was used for the exploitation of resources that, in their view, belonged to the people of their countries. In addition, many of the present-day leaders have been attracted to the socialist model of the economy either through their educational experiences or by being captivated by the apparent successes of the systems used in the Soviet Union and China. Other leaders had backgrounds in the civil service or the military and, therefore, have very little comprehension of economic and business issues. In fact, in several developing countries business activity has not been viewed as an honorable profession compared to some forms of public service, medicine, the legal profession, or the armed forces. In many of these countries, businessmen were considered to be too closely associated with the former colonial powers and some were accused of wanting to maintain the colonial form of government to protect their own economic interests. At the same time, political leaders in the forefront of the independent movements and the postindependence political consolidation period viewed indigenous business groups, especially the large business enterprises, as being too narrow in their outlook and exclusively concerned with the immediate question of profits. This, in turn, made them suspicious of the motives and methods of businessmen.

The attitudes of Third World leadership groups toward MNCs, shaped by their backgrounds and positions held, have been reinforced by the tasks which need to be performed to retain the position of power assumed after independence had been gained. These tasks include the continuous mobilization of citizens to rally around the nation, highly visible achievements in the enhancement of their economic welfare, and a continuous exaltation of the new nationhood, which must not suffer from any apparent infringement upon the independence and decision-making autonomy of the government.   The priority of these tasks implies that the MNC, with its transnational capabilities and large resources, is likely to be regarded as a potential threat to the leadership groups and to the independence of their country since its control may be difficult. Therefore, the obvious benefits for a developing country may be outweighed by the problem of controlling the corporation in such a way as to assure its full acceptance of the broad objectives of the host government. In practical terms, this often means the insistence of the government that ownership of the MNC affiliate be at least 51 percent in its hands, although minority ownership has been accepted at times. Such an arrangement is usually carried out through the country's development corporation, a governmental agency that is the participant in a number of these ventures and supervises compliance with governmental regulations. Of course, these terms are frequently not acceptable to MNCs, and the range of beneficial investments in a given developing country is greatly reduced.

While the attitudes described above are typical, there are exceptions from time to time and in certain countries, often depending on precedents of MNC investments. Moreover, a new, younger generation of governmental leaders and administrators may also adopt a more flexible and favorable view of the benefits of MNC activities. Offsetting these favorable developments for MNC investments in some parts of the Third World are tendencies of private business firms in a given country, despite their commitment to free enterprise, to promote or support government decisions against permitting the establishment of an MNC affiliate if they view this as a threat to their vested interests. In fact, in such a case they may use opposition parties, if they exist, to lobby against admission in the event that the government is seriously considering issuing an appropriate invitation to an MNC.   Their pervasive fear is that new competitive forces brought into the country may compel them to abandon their traditional and often antiquated business policies. Since a widespread regimen of control and regulations operating in many developing countries assured competition to be restricted and profits to flow in easily, it is not surprising that many local businessmen are anxious not to rock the boat. (23)

Two additional dimensions of MNCs' impact on LDC host-country policies must be mentioned which do not spring directly from the nature of MNCs but which, nevertheless, are often strongly rested by Third World political leaders. They are the extraterritorial effects of certain parent country laws and regulations and various efforts by MNC affiliate managements to influence host country policies and laws.

As for the extraterritoriality issues, the best known example is the extension of United States antitrust laws and policies which, although perhaps benefitting some host countries in their struggle to combat monopolistic practices, may run counter to the policies of those countries that might want to encourage mergers. The imposition of export controls by parent governments is another instance of extraterritoriality that can affect the autonomy of host country decision making in several ways. First, it can prevent the importation of goods urgently needed by host countries to implement certain development policies. Second, it may prevent the exportation of certain items manufactured by MNC affiliates in a particular LDC - exports to Cuba by United States affiliates in some Latin American countries come to mind. Third, as already mentioned, controls may be slapped on the export of certain technologies for which one or more Third World country has a special need. All of these problems place into sharp focus the possibility of double allegiance of MNC subsidiaries.

Attempts to influence host-country policies and laws take many forms. While undoubtedly many MNCs want to project or retain the image of the "corporate good citizen" and, therefore, avoid any adverse publicity associated with "lobbying," some corporations and their affiliates have aggressively sought their political ends. Sometimes characterized as "Back Room Heavies," they may engage in large-scale bribery such as paying large commissions or giving gifts to governmental leaders or their families. (24)

Recent, rather painful, disclosures suggest that more than 100 United States MNCs have engaged in these practices to the tune of many millions of dollars a year. Other influencing endeavors include the inducement of concessions by promising to make new investments if certain conditions are met, or threatening the intervention of the parent-company government if the host government takes specific actions or refuses the demands of the MNC. United States companies are not the only ones guilty. In 1965, an Italian constructions consortium probably bribed the Peruvian Minister of development and Public Works along with several Peruvian congressmen to obtain the Mantaro hydroelectric contract, previously assigned to Anglo-German interests. (25)

To achieve their lobbying objectives, MNC headquarters and especially affiliate executives may determine important target groups in the host country with which they maintain continuing relationships. The targets are not only government officials, but also general public and special interest groups, trade unions, news media, shareholders, supplier and customer organizations, universities, and last, but not least, other companies. Functional departments within the MNC and its affiliates are assigned the task of dealing with various target groups. This means that, for example, the marketing department would deal with customer organizations, the personnel department with trade unions, the financial department with shareholders, and the public relations department with the news media and the general public. Some large corporations such as Royal Dutch-Shell or Standard Oil of New Jersey have set up large-scale organizations resembling the foreign ministries of national governments. These organizations engage in carefully coordinated information and intelligence-gathering operations through a network of representatives in the major capitals of the world. At the same time, these representatives are used to present their companies' viewpoints on pertinent issues to the national governments in whose countries they are stationed and seek to influence national decision makers in the direction desired by the corporation management. Periodically, these representatives are called back to headquarters to discuss "foreign policy" problems and to receive new instructions.

To make the lobbying process effective and successful, a variety of frequently overlapping coalitions have to be formed. These coalitions are not limited to intranational groups, but may reach regional and worldwide dimensions. They may be formed vertically, embracing the MNC's customers as well as suppliers and their trade associations and they may reach out horizontally to companies with related or common interests and, again, their trade associations. Of course, the closest common interests and allies for the MNC are the specialized interest groups in their own industries.

Finally, possible allies for MNCs may be national or international labor organizations. However, in view of the very complex, often hostile attitudes of organized labor toward MNCs, which have emerged during the last few years, and the generally weak position of organized labor in the Third World, alliances with labor organizations may be effective only in very specific cases.

The successes of lobbying efforts are always difficult to determine and frequently do not become visible until considerable time has elapsed. In many cases, lobbying agents do not want to trumpet their successes to the world, as such publicity may be counterproductive. Of course, they are also anxious to conceal failures whenever possible. But whatever the outcome, LDC governmental leaders face a smoothly operating, very skillful lobbying and influencing apparatus that presents them with serious dilemmas and may utlimately heighten their resentment against all MNC initiatives, regardless of their inherent merits.

How far do parent-company home governments assist MNCs and their affiliates in achieving their particular policy objectives in LDCs? No general judgment can be made; it rather depends on specific circumstances. The International Telephone and Telegraph Co. case in Chile may be an exception rather than the rule. In the United States, American MNCs are neither extensions nor instruments of the government, nor does the State Department support every interest articulated by and dear to an American MNC. One reason is that the perception of the "national interest" varies in different governmental departments such as State, the Treasury, or Commerce that have significant roles to play in MNC matters. Nevertheless, depending on the influence of individual corporations, national governments are likely to respond to pleas for protection and support, especially if such pleas can be based upon the violation of recognized international law rules including problems arising from cases in which the "Calvo Clause" (26) is involved.

SUMMARY

This brief survey of MNC problem areas, especially in instances when affiliates operate in Third World countries, makes it evident that they are potent sources for tension and friction. Perceptions of management, host governmental leaders, and scholars vary widely as to benefits and drawbacks of MNC operations in LDCs, and these perceptions become even more disparate because of the simple fact that neither benefits nor drawbacks are spread evenly. MNCs indeed create wealth, but they may also contribute to greater poverty; they often increase inequality rather than produce a more equal distribution of welfare. For LDC leaders, their main concerns, and understandably so, are the social and political costs for their countries, and these concerns may obscure the economic benefits. For MNC management, the maximization of profits and enlargement of markets have to be the highest priorities, no matter how much they may be committed to satisfying their social conscience. Thus, conflicts are unavoidable and these conflicts have been aggravated by the disparity between the tremendous economic power of the MNCs and the debilitating weakness of many LDC governments. To obtain some countervailing force, Third World leaders have sought refuge in numbers and have increasingly involved organizations such as UNCTAD and other UN bodies in which their voting strength assured support for their interests and aspirations. The involvement of the United Nations in the MNC-LDC problem areas and conflicts is the subject of our next chapter.

3 United Nations Involvement

In response to demands by a number of governments, powerful labor union federations, certain nongovernmental groups, and even some MNCs, the United Nations Economic and Social Council in Resolution 1721 (LIII), adopted unanimously on July 2, 1972, requested the Secretary General to appoint a

> group of eminent persons...to study the role of multinational corporations and their impact on the process of development, especially that of the developing countries, and also their implications for international relations, to formulate conclusions which may possibly be used by Governments in making their sovereign decisions regarding national policy in this respect, and to submit recommendations for appropriate action.

The resolution further requested the Secretary General to submit the report of the group, "together with his own comments and recommendations, to the Economic and Social Council at its 57th session."

A group of 20 eminent persons was established promptly, held hearings, deliberated from September 1973 to March 1974, and issued its report and recommendations in the summer of 1974. (1) The group consisted of representatives from Western industrialized, developing, and communist countries; its professional expertise ranged from academia to business management and government. The American representatives were Senator Jacob Javits and J. Irwin Miller, board chairman of Cummins Engine Company. (2) The group was aided by a comprehensive study prepared by the Department of Economic and Social Affairs of the United Nations Secretariat entitled Multinational Corporations in World Development (cited earlier), which furnished data, analyzed the problem, and discussed various proposals for action. Relevant documents prepared by the United Nations Conference on

35

Trade and Development (UNCTAD) and the International Labour Office were also available to the group. (3) In addition, more detailed studies on the transfer of technology, taxation, and investment codes were prepared for the use of the Group. (4)

In its task, the group was greatly helped by hearings held during its first two plenary sessions, when it heard testimony and answers to questions from some 50 leading personalities from governments, businesses, trade unions, special and public interest groups, and universities. These individuals were drawn from advanced Western industrial countries, communist states, and the Third World, and represented differing economic and political philosophies. This novel approach for the United Nations proved to be a most useful source of information as well as a valuable occasion to test ideas.

The group was also greatly aided by two consultants: Raul Prebisch, an authority on regional matters and United Nations organizations; and Nat Weinberg, former Director of Special Projects and Economic Analysis of the United Automobile Workers Union (UAW) of the United States and Canada.

This chapter will review and analyze the report of the group and collateral United Nations materials, while the next chapter will evaluate the actions that have been taken by the United Nations so far and that may be projected for the next few years.

THE REPORT

The Frame of Reference

The definition for multinational corporations used in the report is very broad and does not capture some of their essential features. It reads:

> Multinational corporations are enterprises which own or control production of service facilities outside the country in which they are based. Such enterprises are not always incorporated or private; they can also be co-operatives or state-owned entities. (5)

Clearly, the second sentence suggests that the report talks about enterprises rather than "corporations" and covers joint ventures among various economic entities. (6) Moreover, under this definition the establishment of one single manufacturing subsidiary of an essentially national company in a foreign country would make it an MNC. This leaves out such important factors as the principle of allocating company resources generally without regard to national frontiers and common management strategies, and the tying together of affiliated business establishments in different countries for the achievement of corporate purposes. (7) Some students of MNCs require a minimum number of subsidiaries in foreign countries and others place emphasis on integrated production. (8)

The issue of definition is significant because it affects the applicability of the prospective code or codes of conduct. This could be all the more crucial if the codes were to be mandatory on MNCs and perhaps also governments. The average observer regards MNCs as private, profit-oriented enterprises of substantial size. But some state-owned enterprises are also profit-oriented, for example Renault of France. On the other hand, state-owned plants in communist countries are not operated for profit motives, although profitability may be a criterion to measure the skill of their managers. However, if such enterprises engage in multinational functions similar to traditional MNCs, they should be subjected to the codes of conduct. But should national companies be included that have only one branch abroad and do not have the entrepreneurial, financial, and administrative muscle to undertake some of the criticized activities discussed in the preceding chapter? We will return to this issue later.

The report stated correctly that many serious national and international problems caused by MNC operations stem from the rapidly growing internationalization of production; during the last two decades, foreign investments of MNCs and the resulting production of goods have been growing twice as fast as world GNP. Because of this trend during the last two or three decades, and the peculiar nature of MNCs of crossing borders with little impunity, the report identified the following as the main concerns of the deliberation of the group:

> Home countries are concerned about the undesirable effects that foreign investment by multinational corporations may have on domestic employment and the balance of payments, and about the capacity of such corporations to alter the normal play of competition. Host countries are concerned about the ownership and control of key economic sectors by foreign enterprises, the excessive cost to the domestic economy which their operations may entail, the extent to which they may encroach upon political sovereignty and their possible adverse influence on socio-cultural values. Labour interests are concerned about the impact of multinational corporations on employment and workers' welfare and on the bargaining strength of trade unions. Consumer interests are concerned about the possible nationalization or expropriation of their assets without adequate compensation and about restrictive, unclear, and frequently changing government policies. (9)

The MNC Impact on Development

In view of the preoccupation of most United Nations member states with Third World problems, it is not surprising that the first part of the report deals with the impact of MNCs on the development of the poorer countries of the world. As we have already noted, there exists an extraordinary assymetry between the economic power of multinational corporations and the majority of nation-states. While many Third World countries would like to tap the extraordinary resources of multinational corporations for improving the economic welfare of their people, a number of anxieties in the minds of governmental leaders of these countries make their relationship with MNCs a very tenuous one. For example, in the testimony given during the hearings conducted by the group, (10) the question of responsiveness of multinational enterprises to the need of expanded employment was raised again and again. Other questions raised dealt with the reluctance of MNCs to carry out research and development activities in poor countries because both facilities and human skills for research are often lacking. Yet, in the view of a number of witnesses, these countries were in the most dire need to raise technological levels within their borders. A third major issue on the minds of many witnesses during the hearings was the difference in objectives of nation-states and MNCs.

The overwhelming economic power of MNCs has made it difficult for many Third World governments to come up with effective terms for either the establishment of a new subsidiary by an MNC or for the continuation of its operation. Although national governments have the political and legal power to pass and enforce laws limiting the operations of MNCs in accordance with national policies, there is frequently hesitancy on the part of governments to exercise these powers because of the real or perceived costs entailed. As a consequence, negotiations between Third World governments and MNCs are frequently awkward and tend to overplay the anxieties of the governments, resulting in either nonentry by MNCs or curtailment of existing operations. As a result, whatever help multinational corporations could give in serving the purposes of development is lost because of misunderstandings and tensions.

In the hearings of the group, three economic and political philosophies were reflected. One has been identified as the liberal conception of the multinational corporation. (11) Under this conception, the multinational corporation is said to be undermining the nation-state, although governments and MNCs are considered to hold each other at arm's length. Nevertheless, the MNC capability of extracting itself from the confining jurisdiction of individual nation-states is regarded as making it an increasingly independent actor on the international scene. Indeed, since MNCs take a global view of research, marketing, and production, it is argued that their policies and strategies are capable of limiting the sovereignty of nation-states with an ever widening web of economic and technological interdependence. Moreover, since the activities of MNCs are seen as promoting the welfare of the people of the world, the nation-state should turn over control of economic affairs to the MNC and, in due time, to other international institutions better suited to a highly interdependent world economy of which the MNC is the predominant expression.

The second economic and political philosophy reflected during the hearings was the Marxist concept of the MNC. It looks at the MNC as representing the latest expression of capitalist exploitation and imperialism. It is seen as an instrument of the international class struggle supplanting the bourgeois nation-state because it is a more efficient instrument through which the capitalistic economies can dominate and exploit the Third World.   According to the Marxist conception of the MNC, there is an institutional imperative for individual corporations to expand abroad.   The research for foreign investment outlets is regarded to be a function of the law of the falling profit rate, which in turn is caused by the accumulation of surplus capital in advanced capitalist economic systems.   Marxists contend that the Cold War in general and the Vietnam War in particular can be explained in terms of the outward thrust of American capitalism for investment outlets. (12)

Finally, a third group of scholars, reflected less explicitly in the hearings, supported what Gilpin calls the mercantilist conception of the MNC.   Under this conception, MNCs are more similar to the trading corporations of the mercantile era such as the British East India Company during the nineteenth century.   Although it is not claimed that the multinational corporations are the instruments of the governments of the advanced countries, and especially of the United States, it is contended that political and corporate leaders in the United States tend to share overlapping interests and perspectives.   The point is made that following mercantile terms, MNCs assist in maintaining the share of world markets of the United States by securing a strong position in foreign economies and controlling access to all materials.   Moreover, MNCs are frequently major generators of foreign earnings needed to assure American national prosperity and to finance United States military and political commitments overseas.   It is, therefore, argued that through the instrumentality of the multinational corporations, the United States, more than any other advanced country, has attempted and continues to attempt to (a) prevent America's exclusion from world markets and from sources of raw materials, (b) maintain a favorable balance of payments, and (c) enhance its power position with respect to other states. (13)

It may well be that all three philosophical orientations overestimate the political power of MNCs flowing from their economic and global activities and underestimate the resilience of the nation-states.   In fact, the mobilization of the United Nations' resources to defend their interests and to bolster their legal authority to regulate MNC activities within their borders, suggests that many small countries have not given up their fight to stand up against MNC power and to exercise their full sovereign prerogatives, despite their frequent paucity of administrative, evaluative, and negotiating skills.

In the hearings, the question was frequently raised as to whether other means of transnational cooperation than multinational enterprises could be used to aid the development process.   Representatives of the communist countries tended to extol the border-crossing cooperation which had been created between enterprises of different socialist countries, especially the popular democracies in Eastern Europe.   These witnesses suggested that similar cooperation could be extended by socialist countries to Third World countries as well.   However, these statements should be taken with a great deal of caution. Clearly, transnational cooperation among the East European satellites and the Soviet Union, as far as specific enterprises are concerned, has been very limited (14), and it is far from sure that the vistas conjured up by socialist representatives and some Third World representatives can be realized quickly and easily.

The group emphasized in its report that regional arrangements could greatly aid the negotiating power of Third World countries regarding the terms of establishing MNC subsidiaries, but the experiences with regional arrangements in the Third World have been such as to cast doubt upon this statement. Theoretically, there is no question that a regional arrangement such as the East African Community or the Central American Common Market could offer greater attraction to MNCs for marketing products manufactured within the region and that this factor alone would strengthen the negotiating hand of the governments participating in the regional scheme. However, unless the regional units become viable, MNCs might not be impressed with the opportunities and prospects for internal market development.

Nevertheless, the Andean Common Market has produced an investment guide for MNCs that appears to be acceptable to many MNCs despite the fact that control over new subsidiaries eventually will shift into the hands of the governments of Andean countries. However, we should also note that the investment provisions of the Andean Common Market have, in particular instances, been watered down when MNCs, whose entry was considered desirable, balked at the terms offered by the negotiations for the Market. Nevertheless, the utilization of public corporations in Third World countries for holding a large minority or even a majority share of the ownership of new or existing MNC subsidiaries has become more widespread and has formed the basis for the establishment of MNC subsidiaries primarily because this scheme provides a high degree of predictability for the operations of the MNC in a particular Third World country.

Based on its deliberations regarding the impact on development, the group put forth a number of recommendations:

1. Despite the opportunities for Third World countries flowing from MNC operations, the basic aim of the international community must be to increase international public aid to Third World countries to meet the needs of the poorest part of the population in these areas.

2. Host countries should consider setting up centralized negotiating services or coordinating groups to deal with proposals for investment by MNCs.

3. The United Nations should train personnel to assist host countries in their negotiating capacities with MNCs.

4. Developing countries should include provisions in their initial agreements with MNCs permitting the possibility of reducing over time the percentage of foreign ownership.

5. In the initial agreement with MNCs, host countries should make provisions for the review of various clauses of the agreement after "suitable intervals."

6. Host countries should adopt policies toward MNC affiliates similar to those applied to indigenous companies unless specific exceptions are made in the national interest.

7. Third World countries should intensify their efforts toward regional cooperation, in particular in the establishment of joint policies with regard to MNCs. (15)

While most of these recommendations appear to be appropriate to the problems of development and reflect some of the realities of international life, the training of large numbers of United Nations personnel suggested to help in negotiations with MNCs could be counterproductive. In the first place, it would require a new bureaucracy added to the many United Nations civil servants already engaged in development work - a costly enterprise in itself. (16) Secondly, it may well make the United Nations an organization biased more and more against MNCs and the free enterprise system as a whole. Considering the trend in General Assembly deliberations during the last few years, primarily orchestrated by Third World countries, such a development could further undermine the authority and legitimacy of the United Nations in the eyes of many industrialized countries and their populations. Fortunately, the Seventh Special Session of the United Nations General Assembly in September 1975 offers hope that the confrontation between the economically advanced countries of the West and the Third World with respect to the international economic order of the future is giving way to serious endeavors of cooperation. Commenting on this session, former United States Ambassador to the United Nations Daniel P. Moynihan observed:

Perhaps never before in the history of the United Nations has there been so intensive and so genuine a negotiation between so many nations on so profoundly important range of issues. (17)

These issues included the problem of the MNCs in the Third World and especially the transfer of technology, which will be examined in subsequent chapters.

The Impact of International Relations

The group's deliberations extended beyond the concerns with development and, not surprisingly in view of disclosures of bribery and other interventions with Third World Host country governmental affairs by MNC subsidiaries, also focused on the MNC's impact on international relations. While, indeed, some MNCs have used their financial resources and economic influence to intervene in the political and

governmental affairs of host countries to bribe governmental officials
and, in general, to lobby aggressively for their interests, employing all
the leverage at their disposal, (18) most of the 4,000 odd MNCs have
attempted to act as good corporate citizens.

In spite of the lack of evidence to attach the "political intervention"
label to more than a relatively small number of MNCs, the group came
up with two strong recommendations:

> The Group unequivocally condemns subversive political intervention
> on the part of multinational corporations directed towards the
> overthrow or substitution of a host country's Government or the
> fostering of internal or international situations that stimulate
> conditions for such actions, and recommends that, in such an
> eventuality, host countries should impose strict sanctions in accord-
> ance with due process of law of the host country concerned. Home
> countries are encouraged to consider ways of ensuring that their
> investment guarantee schemes do not make these sanctions
> ineffective. (19)

> The Group recommends that host countries should clearly define
> the permissible public activities of the affiliates of multinational
> corporations and also prescribe sanctions against infringements. The
> financial contributions of multinational corporations as well as of
> others to interest groups, should be regulated and disclosed. (20)

Another anxiety of many countries hosting affiliates of MNCs is the use
of these units as tools for the achievement of foreign policy goals of the
parent company. In some cases this may lead to the exertion of
unwarranted influences and even pressures on host governments to
change their orientations and policies. In other instances, however,
MNCs may also be used to bolster or supplement foreign aid operations
of the parent government. Generally, the vast majority of MNC
affiliates operate in both industrialized and developed countries only in
the interest of their own economic objectives, although these objectives
may sometimes be restricted by parent-government laws such as the
Trading With the Enemy Act of the United States. To assure against
any undesirable effects in this context, the group recommended that

> the Economic and Social Council...should call upon countries not to
> use multinational corporations and their affiliates as instruments for
> the attainment of foreign policy goals. (21)

Perhaps the most serious cause for tension between host and home
governments of MNCs is the nationalization of MNC plants and other
facilities in host countries. The key question in these nationalizations
of facilities is the amount of compensation to be paid, the manner in
which it should be determined, and the extent to which home countries
should involve themselves in this issue. According to the
recommendation of the group, host countries should ensure that the
compensation is fair and adequate and that it should be determined

according to due process of law of the country concerned. Arbitration arrangements worked out prior to cases of nationalization should be applied.

While these recommendations are well meant, other points are equally important, as Senator Jacob Javits stressed in his dissenting opinion. (22) For example, compensation must be paid promptly and any nationalization of MNC assets must be nondiscriminatory and for a public purpose.

Another recommendation of the group regarding disputes between multinational corporations and host countries, whether pertaining to nationalization or other issues, is somewhat unrealistic. It stated that home countries should refrain from involving themselves in such disputes and, if serious damage to their nationals is likely, they should confine themselves to normal diplomatic representations. It extols home countries not to use international agencies as means of exerting pressure. It is naive to expect that home countries will simply sit idly by when nationalizations of their MNC affiliates take place. Domestic politics will immediately enter into such a situation, and home governments will be under pressure either directly by MNC managements or indirectly through representatives in various legislatures to do something about these nationalizations. The United States has reduced foreign aid in cases of expropriations, and a recent example of counteraction has been the elimination of the most favored nation clause in dealings with Venezuela, embodied in the United States Trade Reform Act of 1974 when that country expropriated the assets of American oil companies. Perhaps a better solution would be to insist that all countries involved in nationalization disputes should make use of the Center for the Settlement of Investment Disputes established by the World Bank. Another solution may be inclusion of the Calvo Clause in agreements between host countries and MNCs.

Finally, an important recommendation of the group suggested that home and host countries should explore, with the help of appropriate United Nation bodies, the possibility of concluding an international agreement regulating the issue of extraterritoriality of jurisdictions. This is especially important in the case of antitrust legislation, and such agreement would be helpful to avoid misunderstandings and recriminations.

Specific Issues

Certain economic factors and management capabilities peculiar to MNCs were given specific attention by the Group of Eminent Persons. One particular problem examined was that of ownership and control of subsidiaries in host countries. The group believed that each host country should determine the kind of economic activity that could be made possible through foreign investment in the light of its own needs and aspirations. Therefore, it was recommended that host countries should clearly define and announce the areas in which they were ready to accept foreign investments and stipulate the particular conditions for such investment. This means that wherever ownership and/or control was to be shared with MNCs, the share for host countries and MNCs must be determined in advance and any shifts in future ownership or control be spelled out in detail.

Whatever MNC investment is to be made, particularly in developing countries, careful consideration must be given to the impact that this investment and the operations of the prospective subsidiary will have on the balance of payments of the host country. In some cases, alternative methods of financing a project through loans and grants from advanced countries might be preferable.

Transfer of Technology

Without doubt, the transfer of technology to an existing or prospective subsidiary is a crucial issue for any host country. In the Third World it has been a special cause for concern. The lack of advanced technology is seen as a symbol of LDC weakness by governmental leaders and the type of technology that may be brought into a developing country may have significant effects on the pervasive unemployment problems. Several United Nations studies were devoted to this subject during the last few years and conducted mainly by the UNCTAD Secretariat and by UNITAR. (23)   UNCTAD and resolutions by the Sixth and Seventh Special Sessions of the General Assembly have further underscored the importance of technology and its transfer for the Third World. (24) Therefore, it was only natural that the group was very much occupied with the technology problem and recommended that machinery for screening and handling investment proposals by MNCs should be designed in such a way as to permit careful examination of the appropriateness of technology that might be introduced.   In this connection, the nature of the kind of product to be manufactured for the domestic market of the host country also needed to be evaluated.

While in view of the widespread existing unemployment in Third World areas the need for labor-intensive technology in developing countries is crucial and, therefore, the recommendation for appropriate screening   machinery   is   understandable,   in   practice,   this recommendation may not always be workable.   The reason is that government officials, especially in many developing countries, are likely to be unqualified to pass judgment on MNC technology and may opt for labor-intensive technology for domestic political reasons.   This could have the effect of shutting off useful advanced technology and be viewed by the MNC as counter-productive to its own business interests. We will discuss this at greater length later.

Another recommendation of the group with respect to technology reflects concerns of both developed and developing countries.   It suggested that as much research as possible be undertaken through affiliates in host countries and that the affiliates should be permitted to export this technology to other parts of the MNC organization at "appropriate" prices.   The concern with appropriate price has merit because high cost of technology may adversely affect the balance of payments of recipient countries. In turn, low prices could harm the country exporting technology in terms of tax receipts. Whether this recommendation is, in fact, workable is not certain: it will be very difficult to determine a fair price for technology. Moreover, much research for technology can only be carried out in countries where the necessary facilities and skills exist. This is frequently not the case in developing countries.

With respect to importing technology, the group recommended that developing countries should seek means other than direct foreign investment. Licensing or the acquisition of patents are, of course, available; but this road could be more difficult and costly, and less rewarding than taking advantage of MNCs. Although the report recommends that international agencies should help in this task, it may be some time before the proper expertise can be developed in the United Nations agencies for this purpose.

Labor

As regards labor, the group recommended that home countries should not hamper the process by which multinational corporations transfer the manufacturing of labor-intensive and low-skilled products to developing countries. It suggested that the domestic work force displaced by such transfer should be protected through national adjustment-assistance measures. The United States Trade Reform Act of 1974 recognizes adjustment assistance and provides channels and funds for this purpose. On the other hand, the group also recommended the creation of an international social fund that would assist in providing compensation to workers displaced by production decisions of MNCs. It suggested that contributions to this fund should be made by MNCs, a suggestion which may find little sympathy from corporations. Indeed, it would be improper, as Senator Javits commented, that the multinational corporations should be compelled to participate in such a fund while perhaps national corporations would not be asked to do the same.

The final recommendation with respect to employment and labor proposed that home countries prevent multinational corporations from going into countries where workers' rights are not respected, unless the affiliate obtains permission from the government to employ collective bargaining and other measures normal in Western countries. This appears to invite home countries to interfere in the affairs of other sovereign nations, clearly an inappropriate request of the management of a private corporation.

Transfer Pricing

Perhaps the greatest apprehension among developed and developing host countries has been caused by the transfer pricing practices of MNCs that minimize the payment of taxes in a particular country and attach higher price labels in countries whose tax laws are more favorable. The group made two recommendations which are designed to reduce this practice:

> ...home and host countries should enforce "arm's length" pricing wherever appropriate; and should elaborate rules on pricing practices for tax purposes.

> ...home and host countries should introduce provisions into bilateral tax treaties for the exchange of available information, and should consider the feasibility of an international agreement on the rules concerning transfer pricing for purposes of taxation. (25

There is no question that transfer pricing is a real problem and should be regulated on an international basis in order to prevent tax evasion. Prices for goods moving within corporation channels should reflect the proper cost and normal profits as if they were to be sold to an outside purchaser.   On the other hand, when developing countries sometimes restrict the remission of dividends or royalties earned by MNC affiliates, it may be understandable that MNCs seek to circumvent such restrictions through transfer pricing and other devices. (26)

Machinery for Implementation

How did the Group of Eminent Persons plan to translate the more than 50 recommendations into realistic action? (27)   Considering that the United Nations is an organization of sovereign states, would there be a reasonable prospect that national governments would accept a code of conduct applying to them as well as to MNCs? What would be the likely reactions of MNCs to the recommendations that can only be enforced effectively in those countries where they would be embodied in law? Without doubt, the group was fully aware of the problems of implementation. This is reflected in the approach used to come to grips with the pervasive and highly complex issues raised by MNCs.   This approach aimed at:

1. The elucidation and analysis of these issues.

2. The acquisition, collation, and evaluation of pertinent information on the subject matter.

3. Consultation among governments, intergovernmental organizations, and interested nongovernmental parties such as business groups, MNCs, labor, and consumers.

4. The elaboration of legal rules acceptable to all parties and perhaps some kind of code of conduct.

The group recommended that the Economic and Social Council become the United Nations organ mainly responsible to oversee this task. A "full discussion of the issues related to multinational corporations should take place in ECOSOC at least once a year." (28) In order for ECOSOC to discharge its new responsibility effectively, the group proposed the establishment of a Commission on Multinational Corporations which would lay the groundwork for and offer advice on the issues and problems brought to the council and prepare the annual discussion.

The specific missions of the commission were to revolve around various types of solutions for the overall problems discussed above. They also included the exploration of enforcement means if specific agreements or a general accord of MNCs were concluded and the promotion of a program of technical cooperation

> including training and advisory services, aimed in particular at strengthening the capacity of host, especially developing, countries in their relations with multinational corporations. (29)

The group suggested that the commission members would serve for a three-year term. They would be selected, as usual in the United Nations, on the basis of broad geographical representation from developed and developing home and host countries and were to have "relevant backgrounds, including those from politics, public service, business, labour, consumer interests, and the academic profession." (30)

The proposal was endorsed fully by the Secretary General who, in the fall of 1974, established a unit named the Commission on Transnational Corporations. The number of commission members is now 48; the term of office is three years on a staggered basis with elections to membership conducted annually by ECOSOC. 31

In addition to the commission, the group recommended the establishment of an information and research center on MNCs. Its chief task was to be the provision of substantive and administrative services to the commission. In view of the continuing and broad range of activities and the expertise required, it was felt that the provision of such services could be more efficiently organized in a unit especially designed for this purpose. Another reason for this added unit was the pivotal role of information and research in the work of the proposed commission. Throughout its work, the group claimed to be struck by the lack of useful, reliable, and comparative information on many aspects of the subject, and reached the following conclusion:

> The availability of pertinent information is central to many issues, such as restrictive business practices, transfer pricing, and taxation. Making available the right kind of information could well be a most important first step in assisting developing countries in their dealings with mulitnational corporations.

> The availability of pertinent information to developing host countries would tend in itself to strengthen their position in dealing with multinational corporations and thus to redress the inequality of power. On the other hand, without a certain amount of expertise to start with, proper use can not be made of information. (32)

The Secretary General fully agreed that analytical clarification of the multidimensional aspects of MNCs' activities would assist the Economic and Social Council and the proposed subordinate commission in conducting a dialogue among the parties concerned and initiating programs of work and institutional arrangements. At the same time, the dissemination of pertinent information and programs of technical cooperation would strengthen the capacity especially of host developing countries to formulate policies, to evaluate the impact of MNCs on their economies, and to ensure that the activities of MNCs are consistent with national interests and development objectives. In recognition of these needs, the Secretary General established the Information and Research Center (IRC) which performs its functions under the general guidance of the Commission on Transnational Corporations (CTN) and under the administrative auspices of the United Nations Center on Transnational Corporations (CTC), established in November 1975. (33)

The CTC is an autonomous body under the aegis of the United Nations and is headed by an executive director appointed by the Secretary General. Klaus Sahlgren, a Finnish diplomat, became the first CTC director in November 1975. Since the center is involved in activities related to those of other United Nations bodies, a coordinating committee has been set up composed of the heads, or their representatives, of the following units, organs, and agencies: The Department of Economic and Social Affairs, the Office of Legal Affairs, the United Nations Industrial Development Organization, and the International Labour Office. Where the need arises, other agencies in the United Nations system are invited to participate in the meetings. The Executive Director of the CTC is a member ex officio of the coordinating committee.

The IRC plays an important role in the CTC. Its terms of reference are: (a) provide substantive and administrative services to the Commission on Transnational Corporations, (b) collect, analyze, and disseminate information and to conduct research and inquiries as directed by the commission, and (c) organize and coordinate technical programs, especially for host developing countries, in matters related to multinational corporations.

4 Proceedings of
the Commission

Beginning with 1975, the Commission on Transnational Corporations has been meeting annually in different cities. The topics discussed in these meetings were not limited to the formulation of a code of conduct for MNCs. Other topics were the establishment of a comprehensive information system on MNCs, technical cooperation among United Nations agencies involved in studies and work on the operations and practices of these corporations, efforts to arrive at a proper definition of the term MNC, and work on international standards of accounting and reporting by large business enterprises. In addition, the commission had to meet its responsibility of supervising CTC.

The composition of the commission mirrors the membership distribution of the United Nations. Representatives from LDCs comprise two-thirds of its members, while ten members were drawn from the ranks of the Western industrialized countries and five from communist countries. This distribution, of course, has affected the voting pattern whenever roll-call votes were taken, but this has been rare. It has also affected the tone of deliberations in the commission; fortunately, earlier acrimony in the debates has given way to moderation and understanding as the delegates got to know each other and their viewpoints. This trend can be seen in the following brief descriptions of the commission sessions held so far.

THE FIRST COMMISSION MEETING

The Commission on Transnational corporations held its first session at the United Nations headquarters from March 17 to 28, 1975. It was convened in conformity with ECOSOC Resolution 1913 of December 1974 (57th Session), which requested the submission of a detailed work program by the commission with due regard for guidelines of MNCs contained in General Assembly Resolutions 3201 and 3204 (Sixth Special Session) of May 1974, and Resolution 3281 (29th Regular Session) of December 5, 1974. (1)   Eleven meetings were   held in which all members of the commission were   represented except Zambia.   In addition, representatives of the following United Nations Organizations attended: UNCTAD, UNIDO, ILO, FAO, UNESCO, and the IMF.

It is interesting to note that other intergovernmental and nongovernmental organizations sent representatives to this first session. Among the   former   were   the   European   Communities,   the   OECD,   the Organization of African Unity (OAU), and the Organization of American States (OAS).   Among the latter were the Chamber of Commerce of the United States, the International Chamber of Commerce (ICC), the International Confederation of Free Trade Unions (ICFTU, the World Federation of Trade Unions (WFTU), and a few others. Clearly, the interests of all these organizations were likely to be touched by the deliberations and decisions of the commission, and, their concern - as suggested by their participation - was legitimate.

The officers elected by the commission members by acclamation reflected the preponderance of the Third World on this body.   The chairman was a delegate from India, and two vice-chairmen were drawn from the Argentinian and Ugandan delegations.   Another vice-chairman came from Bulgaria, and the rapporteur was an Australian.

Both the group of "77" (Third World countries) and a group of Western delegations (France, West Germany, Italy, the United Kingdom, and the United States) submitted lengthy lists of areas of concern that deserved particular attention in the work program of the commission and the IRC.   Significantly, the Group of "77" list focused on the operation and activities of MNCs and expressed many fears discussed in the preceding chapters, while the Western group concentrated more on the relations between MNCs and governments, including discriminatory treatment of   MNC   subsidiaries,   expropriations,   and   the   type   of investment   climate   prevailing   in   various   LDCs.   The communist countries also submitted a list of issues which, however, was very short, referring only to the negative impact of MNCs on labor conditions, balance-of-payment matters, and the raw materials situation. (2)

An air of confrontation pervaded some of the meetings of the delegates.   (3)   Considering the disparities of economic and political philosophies espoused by the various delegations, this should not have come as a surprise to anybody.   As in other forums during the last few years, the developing countries participating in this meeting were able to present a united front in pressing for a work program reflecting views on MNC-government relations in line with the Charter of Economic Rights and Duties of States and the New International Economic Order adopted by the United Nations General Assembly in December 1974.   This meant that the pre-eminent priority of the commission should be a code of conduct for MNCs compelling them to conform to, and   contributed to the advancement of, the policy objectives of countries in which they operate.

As the result of the deliberations during the first session, the commission mapped out for itself and the IRC a preliminary program of projects in several broad and overlapping categories, including:

1. Preliminary work aiming at the foundations of a code of conduct

2. Establishment of a comprehensive information system

3. Research on the political, economic, and social effects of the operations and practices of MNCs

4. Organization and coordination, at the request of United Nations member governments, of technical cooperation programs concerning MNCs

5. Work leading to a proper definition of MNCs

THE SECOND COMMISSION SESSION

The commission's second session took place in Lima, Peru, during the period of March 1-12, 1976. It was marked by a relatively nonconfrontational atmosphere and achieved its procedural mandate of producing a long-term work program that appears to be reasonable. Of course, actual progress toward the goals of the first session had been small because the first task in 1975 and early 1976 was to set up the organizational and administrative machinery for the CTC and the IRC and to assemble the necessary research staff for the latter body. Nevertheless, some useful initial survey work on the vast MNC literature had been accomplished by the time of the second session of the commission. This material improved analytical insights into the problems to be faced and solved by the CTC.

In the election of officers for the second session, the pattern of geographic distribution was basically maintained. The chairman was from Peru, the three vice-presidents were from Bulgaria, Algeria, and the Netherlands, and the rapporteur was a native of Thailand. Various United Nations specialized agencies and a number of intergovernmental organizations - the European Economic Communities, the OECD, and the OAS - were represented. Several nongovernmental organizations - for example, the ICC and some international labor federations - also again sent representatives.

The results of the deliberations were mainly programmatic and procedural, following closely the concepts adopted in the first session. The highest priority was assigned to the elaboration of a code of conduct, although it was recognized that this task was closely related to the establishment of a comprehensive information service, research on the various effects of MNC operations and practices, and the kind of definition for MNCs that would be accepted. At the same time, the commission did not overlook the need for technical cooperation programs to strengthen the negotiating capabilities of Third World countries and the desirability and feasibility of separate agreements on specific subjects. Work was also to be continued on a proper definition of what constitutes a transnational corporation.

For the formulation of the code it was decided to establish an intergovernmental working group in which at least any four members of the commission from each regional grouping would participate. Obviously, the IRC would play a pivotal role in this endeavor; in addition, ECOSOC was to request the United Nations Regional Commissions to assist. Regional meetings of LDCs were to be scheduled to ensure the complete identification of areas of concern to which the code would have to address itself. Consultants with expert knowledge of MNC operations and practices were to be used and their selection made from business, organized labor, public interest groups, and academia on the basis of balanced geographic and functional representation encompassing all commission member states. The working group's task had to be related to ongoing efforts in developing rules for the transfer of technology, restrictive business practices, and others which were in progress in UNCTAD, and to work on employment issues which were being pursued by the ILO. Finally, the working group had to take into consideration the studies conducted and actions taken by the OECD, the European communities, and other forums.

It was the hope of the members of the commission that an annotated outline of the proposed code could be submitted to the third session of the commission in 1977, to be convened from April 25 to May 6 in New York, but this aim was not attained. This should not have been surprising in view of the manifold missions that the commission had given to the IRC, which had to play an important support role for the working groups' efforts in elaborating the code of conduct, (5) and the very small staff of the commission itself. Indeed, an annotated outline of the code did not take shape until early in 1978.

During the discussion on the code, some delegations expressed the view that it should be mandatory in nature, while others opted for a voluntary code. Of course, the enforcement problem would have to be considered, and a number of delegations felt that the consideration of this matter was premature.

Those wanting a mandatory code thought that a simple declaration of principles would not meet the need to remedy what they considered undesirable practices and would not ensure that MNCs would make a positive contribution to the implementation of the program and establishment of the New International Economic Order and the Charter of Economic Rights and Duties of States. However, others expressed the view that a mandatory code required the creation of international machinery for enforcing compliance which would require consent of all nation states, a very time-consuming process with little prospect for eventual success.

The position taken by the United States regarding the nature and the scope of the code was presented as follows. It must be nonbinding and be balanced with respect to the responsibilities of both MNCs and governments. It should apply to multinational enterprises regardless whether ownership is private, state, or mixed. Those supporting a nonbinding code argued that it could be hammered out much faster and would be preferable, given the wide diversity in national legislation and policy objectives. Once the code was accepted by the commission and generally recognized as useful by the member states and the MNCs, an evolutionary process might be triggered that ultimately would lead to a mandatory concept as a matter of legitimacy and effectiveness. No agreement could be found on this issue, but the commission was urged, nevertheless, to proceed without delay to draft the code reflecting a declaration of political will in this endeavor. (6)

In terms of substance, the positions of the Third World delegations and those of the advanced Western countries remained far apart in certain areas, but the possibility of compromises began to emerge in others. This was clearly demonstrated by an analysis of a rather detailed paper submitted by the commission's Latin American and Caribbean delegations for use as a basis for preliminary work for a code of conduct, when compared with a broad note on areas of concern submitted by some of the Western delegations including the United States. (7) An obviously wide gap was reflected by the demand of the paper that MNCs must be subject to the laws and regulations of the host country, and, in case of litigation, subject to the exclusive jurisdiction of the courts of the country in which they operate. Private agreements on court jurisdictions or resort to arbitration for the settlement of disputes, all permissible under international law and considered highly desirable by the group of advanced Western countries, would be impossible.

Another stipulation in the paper objectionable to the advanced Western countries was an obligation for MNCs to conduct their operations in a manner that would result in increased net receipts of financial resources for the host country. This would be a continuing obligation following the initial transfer of funds and would be measured by the impact of the MNC operations on the balance of payments of the host country. These provisions reflected the well-known apprehension of host countries about excessive repatriation of capital, profits, royalties, and other payments for transferred technology, and about undue restrictions on imports from and exports to other entities of the MNC, including international market allocation among the MNC affiliates. Obviously, these provisions seriously limit the freedom of action for MNC managements and were not acceptable in the broad sweep they were stated. The same also applied to another stipulation in the paper making MNCs not only subject to the host country's national policies, objectives, and priorities for development, but also requiring them to contribute positively to their achievement. This would not only place considerable constraint on the conduct of MNC subsidiaries in the countries concerned, but also necessitate headquarters management adaptation of its corporate global strategy.

Another provision in the paper that aroused the opposition of the Western industrialized countries because of its broad sweep, subjected the MNC "to the exercise by the host country of its permanent sovereignty over all its wealth, natural resources, and economic activities." This would open the door to any kind of nationalization and expropriation measure regardless of agreements between MNC headquarters and local entities or governmental units such as public development corporations. MNC subsidiaries would also be enjoined to operate in such a way as to ensure that nationals of the host country can manage and operate the enterprise at all levels, an obvious prerequisite for successful nationalization and or expropriation by the host country government.

Finally, the disclosure requirements about the MNC as a whole were escalated and disaggregated data sought that would allow "the most exact determination possible of the contribution to the national development" of the host country by the subsidiary. While advanced home countries may agree with a higher level of disclosure, they are likely to defend very strongly legitimate confidentiality of trade secrets and management strategies that do not violate any laws and have been traditionally regarded as fully acceptable. Of course, where the proper dividing line lies may defy precise definition.

Other parts of the Latin American paper were less controversial and agreement on specific points by the Western members of the commission should not be too difficult. The injunction upon MNCs to abstain from all interference in the internal affairs of the states where they operate and from interfering or disturbing the relations between host and other governments could generally be acceptable to Western countries, but also raised a variety of questions in the event of slow or inadequate indemnity when facilities of a foreign MNC are nationalized. Advanced Western MNC home countries are unlikely to give up their traditional rights under international law to protect their nationals in the event of what is perceived illegal action. Differing legal views would have to be reconciled and the solutions clearly spelled out in the code. The same applies to the request that MNCs should not serve as an instrument of the foreign policy of another state or become a means of extending into the host country the juridical order of another state, mostly the MNC home country. Antitrust and certain tax laws are the main cases in point, and these problems also require carefully thought-out and clearly stipulated solutions. Another concern of the Third World, to keep MNCs from engaging in a wide variety of restrictive business practices, is also recognized as a basic evil by the advanced Western countries, but while agreement exists on the undesirable nature of some of these practices (such as tied sales or administered import or export prices of goods moving between subsidiaries of an MNC without regard to cost and normal profit), the precise parameters of some practices need to be defined.

It seems that during the second session of the commission few serious attempts were made to overcome the differences on the substance of the code. Perhaps it was felt that this would interfere with or prejudice the forthcoming deliberations of the intergovernmental working group, which should be allowed to consider afresh the various positions and concerns of the opposing parties. Moreover, the experts drawn into the decision-making process from different universities and nongovernmental organizations needed to be heard and their views evaluated before the working group could actually begin intensive work on an annotated code outline which, in turn, needed to be coordinated with related programs in UNCTAD and other United Nations bodies as well as in the OECD. As it turned out, the working group became, indeed, the main forum for the development of the code, although the complexity of the subject matter and the conflicting positions of the Group of "77" and the Western industrialized nations made forward movement on the code slow and often very cumbersome.

THE THIRD COMMISSION MEETING

Held in New York from April 25 to May 6, 1977, the third commission meeting made little progress. Prior to this meeting, the working group, given the mission to prepare an annotated draft of the code of conduct as soon as posible, had met only twice early in 1977. Thus, time was too short to produce such a draft, although specific suggestions for the annotation task had been made. (8)

As for the top officials for this commission meeting, a similar geographic distribution pattern prevailed among the various delegations as in the preceding sessions; an Algerian was elected chairman. The climate of deliberations was generally harmonious, due in part to the absence of controversial subjects. An exception came from the activites of MNCs in southern Africa. A motion was introduced by 20 developing countries that MNCs should comply with United Nations resolutions demanding cessation of further investments in that area and the dismantlement of existing ones. The motion requested the CTC to collect and publicize information on this matter, which the home countries of MNCs were to report to the commision. Unable to reach consensus and breaking its tradition, the commission proceeded to a vote, and - to nobody's surprise - the motion carried with 36 members in favor (all LDCs and the communist members, including Yugoslavia), four against (France, West Germany, the United Kingdom, and the United States), and seven abstaining (all other advanced Western countries). (9)

Some LDC delegations complained that the roster of MNC experts at the center did not contain enough individuals from the Third World and argued that the geographical representation should be widened without, however, affecting the quality of the services offered by the center. This is, of course, almost like squaring the circle: in most intergovernmental organizations, it is rarely possible to meet both the needs of highest expertise and widest geographic distribution when appointing civil servants. This is all the more problematic when the level of knowledge on a topic such as the MNC and its many aspects differs so greatly between scholars and administrators in advanced and developing countries.

A somewhat related subject discussed was the possible involvement of the center in direct negotiations between MNCs and host countries regarding the establishment of a subsidiary or modification of an existing agreement. Some delegations insisted that, in keeping with the principle of neutrality of the United Nations staff, such involvement would violate the integrity of the center as an impersonal source of advice and greater understanding of MNCs. This seems to be a reasonable and proper position as otherwise we would witness a further substantial proliferation of the already extensive United Nations bureaucracy. On the other hand, helping to strengthen the negotiating skills of Third World personnel by the CTC staff would appear to be an appropriate mission of the center. (10)

Apart from this, the meeting was characterized more by an exchange of information among the commission member states than by the adoption of a large number of decisions. The representatives of UNCTAD and the ILO advised the commission of their work regarding MNC problems. Moreover, the views of the International Chamber of Commerce, the International Confederation of Free Trade Unions, and the World Federation of Trade Unions were heard. (11)

THE FOURTH COMMISSION MEETING

The fourth session of the TNC commission convened in Vienna from May 16 to 26, 1978, under the chairmanship of a Canadian, Ambassador Geoffrey Bruce. Since the intergovernmental working group had still not been able to come up with an annotated draft for a code of conduct, the commission requested that three additional two-week sessions be held by the group before the fifth commission meeting in the spring of 1979 in order to expedite the completion of its mandate. (12)

The subject of South Africa was brought up again. At the initiative of the group of "77", the commission adopted a resolution requesting the CTC to prepare a report on the activities of MNCs in the industrial, mining, and military sectors in southern Africa and on nonwhite trade union recognition by MNCs there. The resolution was adopted by 26 votes in favor, six opposed, and five abstaining. The opposing votes, two more than during the third commission meeting, were cast by Canada, France, West Germany, Switzerland, the United Kingdom, and the United States. The abstainers were Italy, Japan, Netherlands, Spain, and Sweden. (13)

In 1976 an Ad Hoc Intergovernmental Working Group on the Problem of Corrupt Parties had been established a subject in whose regulation the United States was extremely interested and had become the prime mover. The task of this group was being carried out efficiently and successfully, and its work was endorsed by the commission during the session. We will return to this topic when we examine individual issues in the next chapter. The establishment of still another ad hoc working group was recommended. This group was to address the complex field of setting standards of accounting and reporting by MNCs. (14)

During the commission session, the United States reiterated its position as to the nature and scope of the proposed code. It also emphasized that the code should not be used as a basis for discriminating action against MNCs be given equitable treatment in accordance with international law.

The positions of other Western industrialized countries on these issues were basically identical to those of the United States, although some disagreed as to the emphasis on the various points made by the United States government. On the other hand, the delegations of the Third World countries remained strongly opposed to these positions. They continued to insist that the code should be binding in nature and legally enforceable by the home and host governments. Moreover, it should uphold the concept of "permanent sovereignty," meaning the absolute power of a state over its wealth, national resources, and economic activities exclusively in accordance with national law. Finally, LDCs did not think that the responsibilities of MNCs need be balanced by any government responsiblities. The communist countries fully supported the stand of the LDCs. We will return to this subject in the next chapter.

THE FIFTH COMMISSION MEETING AND
WORKING GROUP PROCEDURES

Held in New York from May 14 to 25, 1979, the fifth commission meeting followed an agenda and procedural pattern quite similar to the preceding sessions. The operation and scope of the IRC, accounting and reporting standards, corrupt practices, South Africa, and various aspects of the prospective code were discussed. Perhaps the most important decision of the commission was the acceptance of the report of the working group on this subject which reflected limited progress toward the formulation of the code of conduct in spite of serious obstacles still to be overcome in achieving this goal. Indeed, the working group, representing all members of the commission, had become the salient forum for elaborating the code, and the three two-week sessions in September 1978 and January and March 1979 (the fifth, sixth and seventh such sessions) indicated that the enormous labor of the delegates, ably supported by the staff of the CTC, was beginning to bear fruit, and the light at the end of the tunnel seemed to look a little brighter. But at least three more working group sessions were deemed necessary before the 1980 commission meeting to hammer out the final details of the code.

Part of the success of the working group may well be due to the firm, yet understanding manner of its chairman, Mr. Sten Niklasson of Sweden, and the capable rapporteur, Bernardo Sepulveda of Mexico. In addition, the help provided by the CTC has been invaluable. Much of the group's progress can be attributed to a step-by-step approach: The preparation of working papers in which common elements were identified that became visible during the group's discussions and that were then included in tentative formulations to be used as a basis for further deliberations. However, the new formulations were not considered as agreed texts and, therefore, would not prejudice the positions of the participating governments. Nevertheless, these formulations do reflect points of convergence that have emerged among delegations and, since the formulations are presented in normative language, they aid materially in the development of the code.

The group's appoach was aptly characterized in a statement by the chairman, Mr. Niklasson, at the close of the fourth session (March 20-31, 1978):

> Experience so far also shows that the innovative modalities of work by the working group have proved to be useful. I am referring to the step-by-step approach which started with a list of concerns to be transformed into one common paper, setting out the area of work. The next step was the annotated outline of the Code, the discussion of which led to yet another step, the working document of the Centre on, inter alia, common elements on the basis of which we have been discussing.... The fact that we are working on a set of formulations, which we call common elements, or standards, although it appears that a few of them are not necessarily acceptable as such to all of [the delegates] , it is remarkable, especially considering that this stage of work was reached only in five weeks of work since the Group was created. I do feel we have been able to pursue our tasks without losing sight of our objectives, and what is more important, without sacrificing substance. (15)

It may be instructive to relate in some detail the procedures used during the seventh session of the working group in March 1979. The major basis for deliberation and discussion was ECOSOC document E/C. 10/AC. 2/8 of December 13, 1978, containing the formulations by the group's chairman regarding a code of conduct for MNCs. This document is reproduced in Appendix A. Various brief supplementary working papers were also submitted by the CTC.

The session began with a three-day discussion on the implementation of the code. This was followed by a thorough examination of the chairman's formulations during which each of the 55 paragraphs embodied therein were carefully analyzed and evaluated. This took about five and a half days. Finally, the problem of the definition of the MNC was discussed.

At the beginning of each session in the morning and afternoon, the chairman indicated the paragraphs in the formulations of the code which he wanted to cover. Normally, the cluster of paragraphs to be dealt with pertained to a particular topic such as transfer pricing of consumer protection. He invited the delegates to make their comments on each paragraph with respect to both content and phraseology.

In most cases, the discussions were started by a statement of the spokesman of the Group of "77" who, during that particular session of the working group, was a representative of Tunisia. (The previous spokesman for the Group of "77" had been the representative of Jamaica.) The statement of the Group of "77" was normally the result of a caucus of its membership, which was held almost every day at noon. During this caucus different positions of the members of the Group of "77" were coordinated, and an agreed statement prepared.

In some cases, individual delegates of the Third World countries also spoke, and the delegate from India was especially active and voiced his opinion extensively on many occasions.

For the Western countries, the United States and the United Kingdom appeared to be the most prominent spokesmen, in many instances assisted by the West German delegate. The representative of Switzerland frequently expressed opinions, which often were at some variance with the positions of the United States and the United Kingdom.

The views of the communist bloc were normally expressed by the delegate from the Soviet Union. He usually supported the positions of the Group of "77" which has been, of course, a standing attitude of the communist bloc. In many instances, the East German delegates spoke up and echoed the views of the Soviet Union. Sometimes the Romanian and Czech delegates also spoke in support of the Soviet position.

Before concluding the discussion on this particular cluster or paragraph, the chairman normally called on the expert advisors which were assisting the working group. Many of these individuals were present or past officials of large multinational corporations and a few were representatives of trade unions. For example, among the group of experts was the president of the IBM World Trade Corporation and the secretary general of the Organization of African Trade Union Unity. In addition, statements were made by intergovernmental organizations represented by observers such as the Organization for Economic Cooperation and Development (OECD) and the Commission of the European Communities.

Finally, nongovernmental organizations requested to make statements. For example, the representative of the International Organization of Consumers Union expressed the views of that organization with respect to consumer protection against multinational corporations.

This brief account of the procedures of the working group reflects the very circumspect method used by the chairman. Every paragraph was thoroughly examined, and every delegate was given ample time to express his views on the substance and wording of particular provisions. In many cases, new language proposed by some of the delegates was carefully noted and is likely to find its way into the revised formulations on the code of conduct to be published for subsequent sessions and may end up as a part of the code.

Clearly, this is a very tedious process, but in view of the many conflicting positions that exist within the working group and the commission, it is the only possible way to arrive at an agreed text for the code. The complexity of this process in which the working group is engaged will become much clearer in the next chapter, which discusses the battles about major issues and the positions of individual delegates and major groupings.

5 Issues and Controversies: Substantive Elements of the Code

The task of the working group to formulate a draft code of conduct is very difficult for two main reasons: (a) the interests and aspirations of the Commission member states and their constituencies diverge widely, and (b) some of the features that must be part of the code have already been subject of negotiations and decisions in other bodies of the United Nations. The main examples are the transfer of technology in UNCTAD and employment issues in the ILO.

INITIAL POSITIONS

The enormity of the working group's task can best be seen by the initial positions taken by the Group of "77" and five leading industrialized countries (the United States, United Kingdom, France, the Federal Republic of Germany, and Italy) during the commission meeting in Lima in 1976. There were 21 main areas of concern with respect to MNCs. Although we have discussed some of these in preceding chapters, it is useful to present all of them here again in summarized form in order to appreciate the progress that has been made since 1976. These areas of concern are

1. Preferential treatment demanded by MNCs in relation to national enterprises.

2. Lack of adjustment by MNCs to the legislation of the host countries in the matters, inter alia, of foreign investment and policies concerning credit exchange, fiscal matters, prices and commercial matters, industrial property, and labor policies.

3. The negative attitude of MNCs towards the renegotiation of original concessions when this is considered necessary by the government of the host country.

4. The refusal of MNCs to accept the exclusive jurisdiction of domestic law in cases of litigation.

5. Direct or indirect interference in the internal affairs of host countries by MNCs.

6. Requests by MNCs to governments of the country of origin to intercede with the host government, by means of political or economic initiatives in support of their private interests.

7. The refusal of MNCs to accept the exclusive jurisdiction of domestic law in the question of compensation for nationalization.

8. Extension of MNCs of laws and regulations of the country of origin to the host country.

9. The activities of MNCs as instruments of foreign policy or intelligence work.

10. The contribution of MNCs to maintaining racist and colonial regimes.

11. The role of MNCs in the illegal traffic of arms.

12. Obstruction by MNCs of the efforts of the host country to assume its rightful responsibility and exercise effective control over the development and management of its resources, in contravention of the accepted principle of permanent sovereignty of countries over their natural resources.

13. Tendency of MNCs not to conform to the national policies, objectives, and priorities for development set by the governments of the host countries.

14. Withholding of information of their activities by MNCs, making host countries unable to carry out effective supervision and regulation of those activities.

15. Excessive outflow of financial resources from host countries due to practices of MNCs and failure to generate expected foreign exchange earnings in the host country.

16. Acquisition and control by MNCs of national, locally capitalized enterprises through controlled provision of technology, among other means.

17. Imposition of excessively high prices for imported technology without any adaptation to local conditions.

18. Failure by MNCs to promote research and development in host countries.

19. Obstruction or limitation by MNCs of access by host countries to world technology.

20. Imposition of restrictive business practices, inter alia, on affiliates in developing countries as a price for technical know-how.

21. Lack of respect of the sociocultural identity of host countries. (1)

The industrialized countries listed 23 areas of concern which they wanted to be taken into consideration in the formulation of the code. They are:

1. The extent to which host country legislation and regulations may discriminate, either in favor of MNCs or against MNCs as compared to domestic enterprises, in the treatment of enterprises on the basis of whether or not such enterprises are under foreign control; the extent to which any such discriminatory treatment affects the activities of MNCs as well as the contributions of MNCs to the development objectives of host countries.

2. The extent to which expropriation of properties undertaken for public purposes related to internal requirements of the countries concerned are nondiscriminatory in application and are accompanied by prompt, adequate, and effective compensation.

3. The extent to which recourse to international arbitration, including that provided by the International Center for Settlement of Investment Disputes, or other dispute settlement organizations or procedures play a role in the settlement of disputes arising out of the activities of MNCs.

4. The effect of the presence or absence of a stable investment climate as a factor affecting the ability of MNCs to contribute effectively to development.

5. The observance and nonobservance of contracts and agreements between MNCs and governments, the consequential issues which arise in the case of nonobservance by either party, and the role which contracts may play in the creation of a stable investment climate.

6. The role which freedom or restriction of establishment by MNCs in countries may have in assisting or hampering economic and industrial development.

7. The extent to which domestic laws, regulations and practices on social policies help or hinder development of labor-relations activities in MNCs.

8. The extent to which the social policies practiced by MNCs help or hinder development of labor-relations activities in countries in which they operate.

9. The effects of MNC operations and activities on employment and job creation, and whether these give rise to benefits, e.g., job creation, or nonbenefits, e.g., strain on indigenous resources of host countries.

10. The extent to which the presence or absence of declared points of contact within both MNCs and host governments have assisted or hindered development of an effective and continuing dialogue between the parties concerned.

11. The effect of MNC operations and activities on the social and cultural identities of host countries, the positive or negative impacts which these may have on such countries, and the extent to which host countries make their expectations known in these respects.

12. The extent to which existing codes of conduct and guidelines concerned with any aspect of the range of issues relating to the activities of MNCs, including the study of the materials underlying such codes and guidelines, commentaries thereon and their implementation and/or effects of such codes and guidelines upon MNCs and governments.

13. Issues relating to cooperation between host governments and MNCs to ensure the fullest possible attainment of national development when MNCs invest in host countries, including whether MNCs invest in host countries, including whether MNCs and host countries state their needs and objectives in a sufficiently clear manner.

14. The need to define more clearly the areas of acceptable and unacceptable political activities on the part of MNCs.

15. The role played by MNCs and governments in the transfer of technology to host countries, including the types of technology involved, conditions imposed by MNCs and governments in connection with such transfers, and the positive and negative effects on technology transfers and the framework within which they are made on host country development objectives and the viability of the investment concerned.

16. The role played by MNCs in fostering development and growth of related industries in host countries and the positive or negative effects of the activities of MNCs on the existing patterns of indigenous supply and production.

17. The extent to which MNCs endeavor to participate in or ignore local business and regional organizations of host countries, host country regulation of such participation where these exist, and the consequences of MNC and host country actions in this area.

18. The extent to which MNCs seek to promote indigenization of their operations and activities in host countries, including appointment of staff at all levels, and the extent to which policies adopted by host governments help or hinder this process.

19. The extent to which MNCs may help to improve or make worse the working conditions of employees, including workers' health and safety, and the extent to which host governments make clear their requirements and/or expectations in these respects.

20. Identification of those countries which have declared policies on conservation and protection of the environment, and the extent to which these may or may not be observed by MNCs operating therein.

21. The appropriateness or otherwise of the forms in which MNCs allow

for participation in the equity of their operations in host countries, and relevant host-country policies and the extent to which these are made known.

22. The extent to which MNCs take host countries' interests into account in the repatriation of capital, remittance of profits, payments of dividends, royalties, and management fees, the extent to which the levels at which these are made are constrained by governments, and the effect this may have on the development process.

23. The extent to which domestic commercial policies, e.g., in relation to restrictive business practices, have been developed by host governments, whether appropriate machinery has been set up by them within which MNCs and governments may discuss problems of mutual interest and, if so, the extent to which MNCs and/or governments use these facilities when it would be appropriate for them to do so. (2)

THE SEARCH FOR COMMON ELEMENTS

It was decided early in the deliberations that the code would consist of six chapters: 1, "Preamble and Objectives"; 2, "Definitions"; 3, "Major Principles and/or Issues Related to the Activities of Transnational Corporations"; 4, "Principles and/or Issues Relating to the Treatment of Transnational Corporations"; 5, "Legal Nature and Scope of the Code"; and 6, "Implementation". To overcome the differences in positions, the group turned its attention first to chapters 1, 3, and 4, whose subject matters contained more common elements and appeared to have greater prospects for compromises than chapter 2 and especially chapter 5, where the gap between opposing positions was very wide.

The basic method of operation in the group's deliberations was to set forth with respect to each item for the code the principle and/or issue involved, identify the elements in which agreement existed, list other points raised by some group members, and add commentaries of a legal or organizational nature, for example whether a particular code provision should be in one or another chapter. The discussion of issues that had been dealt with in other forums, such as transfer of technology (UNCTAD), employment and labor (ILO), and corrupt practices (ad hoc working group), was initially postponed. Without doubt, this approach, although slow, was systematic, useful, and effective.

The first major attempt in producing an annotated code elaborated by the commission staff was published in January 1978 for the third session of the working group held in February of that year. (3) It showed a beginning, although modest convergence of viewpoints between the developed and developing countries. At the March 1978 session of the group (its fourth meeting) the CTC presented another annotated draft code in the form of a working paper. (4) This paper reflected considerable work by the participants of developed countries and LDCs and, in the view of the industrialized states, seemed to be more balanced than the preceding effort. However, the reactions of the Third World and communist representatives were negative with respect to many of the provisions and concepts contained in this draft.

A concrete example of how this procedure of preparing an annotated draft code looked in print may be instructive, and I have chosen for this the issues of taxation in chapter 3, as presented in the working paper produced by the CTC. The treatment of taxation during the proceedings was relatively short; with respect to other issues which were more controversial, many other points were raised, several tentative formulations of common elements undertaken, and several, often extensive, commentaries offered.

Taxation

Annotations

    a) Provision by transnational corporations of relevant information to government authorities subject to suitable safeguards with regard to confidentiality

    b) Account to be taken of work conducted by the United Nations Group on Tax Treaties and the role of bilateral and, as appropriate, multilateral tax treaties.

Common Elements: Tentative Formulation

Transnational corporations should refrain from using their transnational structure and operations to evade taxation or substantially reduce the tax base in the countries in which they operate by employing transfer-pricing principles, intracorporate payments and royalties and fees and other similar financial transactions beyond accepted commercial practice for domestic enterprises in comparable situations.

Transnational corporations should, in accordance with laws, regulations, and administrative practices of the countries in which they operate, disclose to the appropriate authorities all relevant information needed for tax assessment, subject to suitable safeguards regarding confidentiality.

Other Points Raised

It was suggested that issues of taxation and transfer pricing be treated together, as the main method of governments to cope with transfer-pricing problems is by way of taxation.

Commentary

The importance of intergovernmental cooperation was stressed. In this context the importance of bilateral and multilateral treaties was strongly emphasized. These would include the treatment of double taxation and tax evasion as well as exchange of information among tax authorities. The work of the United Nations Group of Experts on Tax Treaties was endorsed.

It is important to understand that the tentative formulations of common elements in the working paper were not considered as an agreed text and did not prejudice the positions of the working group members. They served as a basis of further discussion and were important in the process of developing the code because they were written in normative language and reflected points of convergence that had so far emerged among the delegations.

The initially very slow progress of preparing a draft code generated rumors that some countries had been losing interest in the whole enterprise. However, later the careful step-by-step approach employed by the working group was recognized as useful, and during the meeting of the group in March 1978 representatives of several countries, including the LDCs, communist governments, and the United States, emphasized their strong interest and commitment to completing work on the code. The United States Representative also specified the manner of adoption that he thought should be consensus. (5)

A further significant step was taken by the working group at its September 1978 meeting (fifth session), when it authorized its chairman to draft formulations for a future code which would attempt to consolidate the discussions of the working group so far. These formulations (6) were presented to the sixth session of the working group in January 1979, but not fully debated until the seventh session in March of that year. They were a tremendous step forward toward the actual articles.

THE CODE FORMULATIONS

The working-group chairman's formulations regarding a code of conduct covered chapters 3 and 4 of the agreed outline relating to the activities of MNCs as well as their treatment. There were 35 paragraphs devoted to MNC activities under these general headings: (A) "General and Political", (B) "Economic, Financial and Social", and (C) "Disclosure of Information". Eleven paragraphs addressed themselves to the treatment of MNCs; the headings of these categories were: (A) "General Treatment of MNCs by the Countries in Which They Operate", (B) "Nationalization and Compensation", and (c) "Jurisdiction." Finally, two paragraphs contained provisions on "Intergovernmental Cooperation."

In an introductory note, the group's chairman assumed full responsibility for the form and contents of the formulations and declared that they did not commit the delegations in any way. Since the legal nature of the code had not been agreed upon and, therefore, specific commands to the parties involved would have been inappropriate, the word "should" instead of "shall" was used throughout the formulations. This suggested that the formulations were primarily a basis for deliberations rather than the draft for a code. One exception to this principle was made with respect to the two paragraphs dealing with intergovernmental cooperation. The reason was that this concept had received broad support in the discussions held in the various sessions of the group and agreement in this matter was considered of fundamental importance to ensure the effectiveness of the prospective code of conduct. Hence, the word "agree" was seen as the most appropriate term for the two paragraphs.

While it would exceed the scope of this volume to examine in detail each paragraph of the formulations, a brief analysis and comments on the provisions in the various sections of the document may offer insights into the general tenor and thrust of the endeavor. (The full text of this document appears in Appendix A.)

General and Political MNC Activities
(Paragraphs 1-16)

The subtitles preceding various clusters of paragraphs in this section suggest that many concerns of the Group of "77" were taken into consideration. "Respect for national sovereignty and observance of domestic laws, regulations, and administrative practices" (paragraphs 1-3) by MNCs is emphasized and the exercise of full permanent sovereignty over a state's resources and economic activities is stressed. In particular, the right of the government to regulate and monitor MNC activities operating within the state's boundaries should be respected. While this is normally accepted, dilemmas may arise for MNC managements when home and host countries issue conflicting regulations; the question arises: which activity is entirely within or outside a state's boundaries? Despite the fact that these paragraphs strongly support the concept of national sovereignty, some LDC delegations claimed the states' right to exercise jurisdiction over MNCs should be strengthened. Others, mainly in the Western group, felt that these provisions should fall under "Treatment of Transnational Corporations," be more balanced, and contain references to international law and contractual obligations.

Another LDC aspiration embodied in the formulation is "adherence to economic goals and development objective, policies and priorities" by MNCs (Paragraphs 4-5). However, there is an important qualification in paragraph 4, inasmuch as this adherence must be consistent with the need of the MNC entity to maintain the viability of its operations. If this is assured, the MNC subsidiary should make a "positive" contribution toward the attainment of the economic goals and development objectives of the countries in which they operate, particularly

LDCs. Effective participation on the national and, where appropriate, on the regional level to further development is urged upon MNCs, something which, despite consultation with governmental authorities, may not always be possible and so would lead to tensions and conflicts. There was disagreement on the part of LDC delegations regarding the reference to "viability" as introducing an unjustified qualification.

With a view to achieving the development goals, MNCs should also respond favorably to governmental requests for "review or renegotiations of contracts concluded...in circumstances marked by duress, or clear inequality between the parties or where the conditions...have fundamentally changed..." (Paragraph. 5). Obviously, such a provision would introduce enormous uncertainties in the relations between MNCs and governments despite the appeal to fairness (who would determine what is fair?) and to the applicable and generally recognized legal principles contained in this paragraph.

In the same vein is the call to MNCs to adhere to "Sociocultural objectives and values" especially important to Third World countries. Again, consultation is advised to avoid activities distorting basic cultural patterns or having undesirable sociocultural effects beyond those necessitated by the introduction of new technologies or by the economic development process itself. Such injunction is very vague and brings about intolerable uncertainties for the management of MNC subsidiaries.

Although another subtitle, "Respect for human rights and fundamental freedoms (paragraphs 7-9) is not always a high priority item for Group of "77" countries, it was found to be generally acceptable; paragraph 9 speaks of noncollaboration with racist minority regimes in southern Africa. This, of course, is a prime concern of the LDCs and, as we have seen, has been the subject of a favorable vote during the third and fourth sessions of the commission. In the view of those governments which opposed this action (including the United States), or abstained from the vote, this may be precisely the kind of political interference which the next paragraph, number 10, basically disapproves.

Indeed, the next subtitle, "Noninterference in Internal Political Affairs," is clearly a major objective of not only the LDCs, but also of the advanced Western countries if subversive methods are employed. However, if such methods are not used, MNC subsidiaries or affiliates have the right in pluralistic societies to participate in the political process and to influence public policy, even if the goal is to change existing legislation or established practice, which is frowned upon by paragraph 11.

The next subtitle for four paragraphs, "Noninterference in Intergovernmental Relations," has much broader implications than the preceding subtitle and reflects the pervasive apprehension of Third World governments about encroachment on their authority and autonomy through the transnational connections of MNCs. In too broad a sweep, paragraph 12 enjoins MNCs from interfering in "affairs which are properly the concern of governments," without stating what is meant by "properly." According to paragraph 13, MNCs should refrain from acting as instruments of a government's foreign policy unless this is done within intergovernmental cooperative arrangements involving the countries in which the MNC entities operate. LDC proponents of this paragraph may overlook that MNCs may be used by home governments for foreign aid purposes, clearly beneficial to the interests of an LDC host country. This paragraph may also be duplicated by paragraph 49, to be discussed later.

In paragraph 14, MNCs are enjoined from requesting home governments to act on their behalf if such action exceeds normal intergovernmental intercourse and amounts to the use of economic and political pressure. Some delegations opposed all references to diplomatic protection, but provisions of MNC home country law cannot be ignored and such law may provide for termination of aid in cases of uncompensated expropriation, as prevails in the United States. This kind of dilemma needs to be recognized by the code.

Finally, for the resolution of disputes, MNCs should exhaust, in accordance with "international standards," the means provided by local law in the countries in which they operate or by other agreed means before seeking diplomatic protection from their home countries (paragraph 15). While this paragraph implies a limitation of the Calvo Clause, it is somewhat ambiguous. Suggestions were made during the seventh working group session to replace "standards" with "law and practice" and add "consular" protection as a final resort. On the other hand, several LDC delegations wanted to limit protection of home governments in both paragraphs 14 and 15 and this stand was supported by the communist delegation.

The last subtitle dealt with "abstentions from corrupt practices" (paragraph 16), but since this topic had been turned over to an ad hoc Intergovernmental Working Group on the Problem of Corrupt Practices, no formulation of a text was attempted. We will discuss this topic in the next chapters.

Economic, Financial, and Social Issues
(Paragraphs 17-42)

Under the subheading "ownership and control," paragraphs 17-20 admonish MNCs to be "good corporate citizens" and, as was already stated in preceding paragraphs, to contribute to the economic and social development of the countries in which they operate. For this purpose, various units of MNCs should cooperate with each other as well as with home and host governments and nationals of these countries, especially if the latter are local partners.

These provisions may well be somewhat weak from the perspective of the Group of "77" as was pointed out by the representative of Tunisia. (The author was an observer during part of the working group session.) On the other hand, some of the delegates of the developed countries complained that the formulations were too vague and lent themselves to conflicting interpretations, although they were deemed to be generally acceptable.

Paragraphs 20 and 21, still under the same heading, urge MNCs to give priority to the employment and promotion of nationals of host countries at "all levels of management and direction." Moreover, in order to assure this goal, MNCs should introduce appropriate managerial training programs. These provisions meet long-standing desires of the LDCs and were approved by the spokesmen for the Group of "77." For some delegates of the Western countries, the phrase "at all levels of management" appeared to be too broad. However, this phrase can only apply to the host country entity, and host country authorities must realize that this goal may take considerable time to be attained.

The subsequent six paragraphs relate to the critical problem of "balance of payments and financing." MNCs are requested to promote exports of host countries, aid in the diversification of production for exports, and use as much as possible the goods, services, and other resources of these countries. This is a generally reasonable request assisting the balance of payments of a host country which, moreover, is cushioned by a qualifying clause that the viability of the MNC units must be maintained. However, the remittance of profits from subsidiaries, the repatriation of capital in case of disinvestment, and other short-term movements can cause problems. Paragraphs 24 and 25 seek to restrict such actions when they might aggravate existing serious balance-of-payment difficulties of host countries. Paragraph 26 imposes a similar general restriction on border-crossing transfers of goods, services, or funds between corporate entities. In all three provisions are qualifications permitting MNC actions that fall within generally accepted commercial practice and, thereby, give increased latitude to MNCs. LDCs have objected to these qualifications and were supported by the communist countries. From the Western side, it was asserted that the vague prohibition against MNCs influencing the imports and exports of local subsidiaries could be unworkable in practice and that perhaps MNCs are being shouldered with too much responsibility for balance-of-payment problems. It should be noted that numerous bilateral and multilateral treaties deal with the question of capital in case of disinvestment and income from invested capital. Moreover, at the Conference on International Economic Cooperation (CIEC) in 1976, it was agreed that timely and unrestricted transfer from investment capital and repatriation of such capital when the investment is terminated is one of the principles that will contribute importantly to a stable climate for private foreign direct investment. While there was consensus that balance-of-payment difficulties were a valid ground to limit such transfer, the LDCs wanted a broad right to take appropriate remedial measures, while the Western industrialized countries insisted that such measures should be exceptional and of limited duration. Perhaps the best formulation for an appropriate provision would be the one suggested by the CTC which reads:

> Transnational corporations should, in accordance with national laws and international obligations freely subscribed to by the

countries in which they operate, be permitted timely and un-restricted transfer of capital in case of disinvestment and of income from investment capital, unless such transfer could aggravate serious balance-of-payments problems of such countries. (7)

Paragraph 27 seeks to protect the availability of local capital markets for national enterprises by using MNCs to refrain from financing activities that might adversely affect the functioning of such markets. This may raise the question of discrimination of MNC subsidiaries, which will be examined in more detail later.

To avoid frictions, paragraph 28 recommends that MNCs consult with host governments to coordinate actions aimed at alleviating balance-of-payments and financing problems.

Paragraphs 29-31 are devoted to the very sensitive issue of transfer pricing. MNCs are enjoined from using pricing "principles, which, contrary to national legislation and policies," may modify the tax base, avoid exchange controls, or adversely affect competition, technological development, and employment in the host and home countries (paragraph 29). In a more positive sense, paragraph 30 requires MNCs to use pricing methods based on "international market prices, or, in the absence of such prices, the 'arm's length' principle." For the Group of "77," these provisions are not comprehensive enough and should include pricing "policies" and "practices." Moreover, the emphasis should be primarily on the "arm's length" principle. The question was also raised how far transfer pricing would respond to legislation. Some of these suggestions were accepted by the Western delegations, which, on the other hand, recommended elimination of references in paragraph 29 to "competition, technical development, and employment."

To determine what kind of pricing principles are employed by MNCs, paragraph 31 requires disclosure of all relevant information to governmental authorities. This may be a duplication of paragraph 41 which is more comprehensive. Disclosure must also be limited by the legitimate need for business confidentiality, especially if it might have adverse effects on the firm's competitive posture.

The formulations on "taxation" (paragraph 32) did not come from the group's chairman because most of the relevant work was done by the Group of Experts on Tax Treaties in the United Nations. Therefore, the CTC was asked to prepare an appropriate formulation. Paragraph 32 addresses itself mainly to the need for MNCs to furnish all relevant information for tax assessment and to the avoidance of tax havens and intracorporate pricing not based on the arm's length principle. Apart from minor disagreement, the delegates basically accepted this pro-vision, although the United States representative drew attention to the need for business confidentiality as a limitation of information disclosure.

Paragraphs 33-35 are assigned to the following subjects: "Competi-tion and Restrictive Business Practices"; "Transfer of Technology"; and "Employment and Labor." Since these subjects have been dealt with extensively in UNCTAD and the ILO, they will be examined in the next chapter as specialized components of the code. No text is provided in the chairman's formulation for these paragraphs.

"Consumer Protection," highly topical in the industrialized societies of the West, also is a major concern in the code formulations (paragraphs 36-39). MNCs should be obligated not to endanger the health and safety of consumers through their operations and products and should not lower the quality of their products to the detriment of consumers. The guidelines for consumer protection are to be found in national laws, regulations, administrative practices, and policies of the countries in which MNCs operate as well as in international standards. Paragraphs 37 and 38 contain very broad disclosure requirements regarding MNC products and services, including appropriate warning measures taken by them and the labeling and advertising methods used. Finally, according to paragraph 39, MNCs should cooperate with host and home governments and intergovernmental organizations in the development of national and international standards for broad consumer needs and protection.

The Western industrialized countries raised two basic objections: (a) the disclosure requirements are much too broad, and (b) national firms must be subject to the same provisions as MNCs. Otherwise, a serious case of discrimination would exist. As for specific labeling and other regulatory measures, they should be dealt with by individual governments and intergovernmental cooperation. However, most developing and communist delegations opposed inclusion of national firms in the code provisions on consumer protection and, in fact, wanted to strengthen these provisions for MNCs further. This clearly demonstrated Third World bias against MNCs and reflected the protective hand of LDCs over their national firms, although this makes little sense considering that consumer protection by its very nature is indivisible.

Code provisions on "environmental protection" (paragraphs 40-42) are similar to those of consumer protection and also contain extensive disclosure requirements which, in their broad sweep, are objectionable to the Western industrialized countries. Otherwise, basic agreement was expressed by all delegations.

Disclosure of Information
(Paragraphs 43-44)

The fact that the two paragraphs dealing with disclosure of information rate a separate subheading may reflect the serious concern, especially of LDC governments, that secrecy of operations is a major element in the power of MNCs and that such secrecy must be fractured if governmental authorities are to exercise a measure of control over MNC activities. As a consequence, paragraph 43 requires periodic "clear and comprehensible information designed to improve understanding of the structure, activities, and policies" of the MNC as a whole to the public at least once a year. Such data are in addition to the information required by the governmental authorities under national laws and administrative practices and should extend to all phases of financial and operational activities, not only of the subsidiary in a particular country, but also of all other activities of the MNC. An illustrative list of items is given in paragraph 43 (see appendix), but obviously other items could be added by governmental authorities. An Ad Hoc Intergovernmental Working Group of Experts on International Standards of Accounting and Reporting may provide further guidance in this respect. Finally, paragraph 43 stipulates in detail the method of how the requested information on the MNCs' various, worldwide operations are to be broken down.

Paragraph 44 extends the information search by requesting all information that governments might need for legislative and adminis- trative purposes relevant to MNC entitles within their boundaries as well as in other countries and necessary to assess the performance of local units.

While much of the data sought is fully justified, the information net is cast too wide and the catchall clauses of paragraph 44 are clearly unacceptable as indicated by some Western delegations. Perhaps some reference should be made also to confidentiality of certain business information. In any case, to reach agreement on this subsection will be difficult, since a direct clash of basic interests and philosophies between LDCs and the developed market economy countries is involved. This is demonstrated by the request of several LDC delegations that a distinction should be made between information disclosed to govern- ments, which should be given on a regular basis and not only on specific requests, and that disclosed to the public. In fact, it was suggested that the formulations deal first with the disclosures to governmental authorities. Others wanted to make distinctions on the basis of MNC size in determining the amount of information disclosed to the public.

There was broad understanding for the inclusion of a provision on the disclosure of information to trade unions, which will be examined in the next chapter when we discuss the ILO involvement.

Treatment of Transnational Corporations
(Chapter 2)

General Treatment of MNCs by Host and Home Countries
(Paragraphs 45-51)

While the provisions in the preceding chapter were addressed to MNCs to solicit their desired behavior, this chapter is addressed to host and home governments setting parameters regarding the application of public policies, laws, and administrative practices vis-a-vis MNCs. Of course, the sovereign power of states to establish conditions for entry of MNCs, limit their activities in specified sectors, and determine their role in economic and social development cannot be abridged by the code; and this is confirmed in paragraph 45. However, according to paragraphs 46 and 47, MNCs should be given "fair and equitable treatment" that is "consistent with national needs to maintain public order and to protect national security," and they should be granted nondiscriminatory treatment in accordance with national laws and administrative practices as well as freely subscribed international obligations in situations "comparable to those of domestic enterprises." Perhaps to strengthen both provisions, reference should also be made to consistency with international law, as was suggested by Western delegations. Other delegations, especially those of LDCs, however, thought that references to fair and equitable treatment of MNCs was not necessary, since this idea could be covered by according MNCs the same treatment as given domestic enterprises under comparable situations. These delegations also opposed references to international obligation or law because they may imply limitations to national sovereignty.

Paragraph 48 urges host and home governments to aim at clarity and stability of national policies and laws affecting MNCs, because this would promote mutually beneficial relations. While nobody can argue with this admonition, the second sentence of this paragraph may well be controversial. It seems to suggest unilateral changes on the part of governmental authorities in agreement with MNC entities when they are deemed necessary "in the light of evolving circumstances." Such action should only be permissible if it is provided for in the agreement in the event of such circumstances or otherwise require mutual consent. Indeed, some Western delegates wanted to include in that section provisions regarding timely and unrestricted transfer of capital from disinvestment and income, but others opposed this as it might unbalance their section of the code.

Paragraphs 49 and 50 repeat injunctions to home and host governments that were in the preceding chapter given to MNCs. Corporations should not be used as instruments for the attainment of foreign policy objectives unless such action is in accordance with intergovernmental cooperative arrangements - perhaps foreign aid - or with "concerted actions of the international community," which may refer to some kind of United Nations or regional IGO activity. If a government decides to intervene with another government on behalf of an MNC, economic and political pressure should not be used and local legal remedies should be exhausted before engaging in diplomatic action and the submission of international legal claims. These are reasonable provisions in accordance with accepted international law, but not quite satisfactory to all LDCs.

Finally, governments should safeguard the confidentiality of information submitted to them by MNCs. Otherwise the competitive position of the MNC furnishing confidential data would well suffer.

Nationalization and Compensation (paragraph 52)

Nationalization is the ultimate weapon of governments, especially in LDCs, to impose control over MNC entities, although its full effectiveness depends on indigenous management capability. According to paragraph 52, it should be carried out only if necessary in the public interest and in a "fair and equitable" manner with considerations of "due process of law" and nondiscrimination. "Just" payment must be made and international obligations and contractual undertakings should be respected.

An annex to the chairman's formulations contains an extensive commentary to paragraph 52. Recognizing the extensive controversies about the legal rules applying to nationalization, it points out that the text of paragraph 52 seeks to reflect those areas where general agreement appears to exist. It would exceed the scope of this volume to delve into the legal intricacies regarding the nationalization process discussed in the annex. Suffice it to say that from the Western perspective, it suggests a proper approach to a complex legal and political problem. Assuming that "just" payment means adequate compensation, perhaps the one element clearly missing from the text is the need to make compensation promptly, a standard espoused by the United States.

On the other hand, the LDCs have different complaints. According to them, the grounds for nationalization should be broadened to include specifically national security and social interest. They opposed the reference to "fair and equitable" treatment and would like to substitute the concept of appropriate compensation for "just" compensation. The nation of "due process of law" may not be applicable, since nationalization measures would not in all cases be subject to further legal procedures. Nor did these delegations see any need for references to nondiscrimination, international obligations, and contractual undertakings because national laws and administrative practices would govern the nature and modalities of compensation. As the formulation stands now, it would impose too heavy a burden on the right of states to nationalize foreign property. (8)

It is then evident that a wide gap separates the Group of "77" and the Western industrialized countries on the procedures and legal standards of nationalization. Bridging this gap will be difficult. However, one must keep in mind that often appropriation cases are settled amicably, and an analysis of these cases may yield a pattern of precedents that might aid in coming to an agreement.

Jurisdiction (paragraphs 53-56)

The subject of jurisdiction is a highly sensitive one for the members of the Group of "77" who want to ensure to the utmost the exclusive competences of national courts over disputes involving MNC entities. This general principle is stated in paragraph 53, but the somewhat ambiguous text could be improved by phrasing it in the singular: "An entity of an MNC is subject to the jurisdiction of a country in which it operates." An exception is stipulated in paragraph 54 for disputes which the state's government "has agreed to settle by arbitration or by other methods of dispute settlement." However, a further exception must be recognized in cases where justice is denied to an MNC entity by a host government. In such an event, international law authorizes the home government to take up the dispute.

Paragraph 55 refers to the choice of law or of the forum for settlement of disputes in contracts involving MNC entities. This choice is to be determined "by the national law of the countries concerned," which is an ambiguous clause in need of clarification. Finally, according to paragraph 56, in the event of conflicts of jurisdiction, "mutually acceptable principles and procedures, bilaterally or multi-laterally," are to be used for the settlement of such conflicts.

There was general agreement in the group that the present formulations could be a useful basis for further discussion, although conflicting views were expressed on the scope of these formulations. Some delegations felt that the elements in this section required further clarification, while others wanted to avoid the elaboration of numerous specific standards. Without doubt, full consensus on this issue of jurisdiction will require compromises and on any sensitive issue. These may not be easy to achieve.

Intergovernmental Cooperation
(Paragraphs 57-58)

As paragraph 56 makes obvious, intergovernmental cooperation is essential if the manifold problems that might arise from MNC operations in different countries are to be resolved satisfactorily. However, whether the provisions dealing with such cooperation should be included in chapter 4, which covers the treatment of MNC entities by home and host governments, is not clear and has been questioned by some delegations of the working group. Consequently, the two paragraphs dealing with this topic have been added to the chairman's formulations under a separate heading and might later be included under chapter 6, "Implementation." Indeed, this might be more appropriate because while paragraph 57 makes a general, more or less self-evident, statement, (9) paragraph 58 touches on the effectiveness of the code, a complex problem which will very much depend on the code's legal nature and its scope, matters that are far from determined, as we will see in chapter 7. Moreover, a subsequent working paper (10) has enlarged on the extent of intergovernmental cooperation and its content is very relevant to the issue of implementation.

SUMMARY

Nevertheless, despite these and other difficulties and future obstacles, the working group discussions of the chairman's formulations show distinct progress over the initial positions put forth by the major groupings of countries involved in the preparation of the code of conduct. Although this progress has been halting and slow, it is a remarkable achievement, considering the ideological bias and sometimes emotional engrossment of some of the participating governments. Of course, whatever progress has been made, it was disappointingly slow for the Group of "77," while the Western advanced countries took the delays in stride and some may perhaps welcome them. Nevertheless, as the discussions moved on, some compromises were reached on conflicting viewpoints regarding the substantive elements of the code, either in the plenary sessions of the group or in private conversations, and this is encouraging. This acceptance of compromises also has marked the negotiations on such specialized components of the code as corruptive practices, the transfer of technology, and labor problems.

6 Issues and Controversies: The Specialized Components of the Code

Several topics that will be included in the prospective code of conduct have been discussed and tentative provisions elaborated outside the Intergovernmental Working Group in special United Nations bodies. We should note that the general scope of these topics exceeds the focus of the code for MNCs, in as much as it encompasses national firms and other international enterprises. However, the deliberations regarding these topics have definite relevance for the code. We will examine these topics in the order in which they appear in the working group chairman's formulations and begin with the issue of corrupt practices and bribery in international commercial transactions.

ABSTENTION FROM CORRUPT PRACTICES

In December 1975, United Nations General Assembly Resolution 3514 (XXX) requested that the Commission on Transnational Corporations address itself to determining measures against corrupt practices by MNCs and other corporations and their intermediaries. During the second session of the commission, many delegations called for immediate action to put an end to such practices. It was also argued that all governments take necessary measures, including legislative action, to prohibit and penalize the illegal acts of MNCs perpetrated within their jurisdictions, and that uniform legislation in several countries could produce uniform legal rules. In particular, MNC home countries should require the disclosure of all payments that bear on the production and sales activities in foreign countries regardless of whether subsidiaries are located in these countries.

The United States delegation proposed the negotiation of a multi-lateral international agreement to deal with all corrupt practices. It suggested the establishment of a working group for this task. The agreement was to be based on the following principles:

1. It would apply to international trade and investment transactions with governments, i.e., government procurement and other governmental actions affecting international trade and investment as may be agreed.

2. It would apply equally to those who offer or make improper payments and to those who request or accept them.

3. Importing governments would agree to (a) establish clear guidelines concerning the use of agents in connection with government procurement and other covered transactions, and (b) establish appropriate criminal penalties for defined corrupt practices by enterprises and officials in their territory.

4. All governments would cooperate and exchange information to eradicate corrupt practices.

5. Uniform provisions would be agreed for disclosure by enterprises, agents, and officials of political contributions, gifts, and payments made in connection with covered transactions.

The commission decided to forward this proposal to ECOSOC and recommended that the matter of corrupt practices be considered on a priority basis with appropriate action to be taken by the 1976 fall session of ECOSOC.

While everybody will declare himself to be against corruption, it was naive to expect quick agreement on the multilateral agreement proposed by the United States no matter how much priority treatment will be given by ECOSOC and the General Assembly. Bribery, kickbacks, and large gratuities concealed as "commissions" have been part of the commercial scene for centuries. Standards of public morality vary from country to country, and high government officials in home and host countries that have benefited from these practices, sometimes as a matter of custom and tradition, were likely to find many bureaucratic reasons and means to delay or obviate the negotiation of such an agreement on the part of their government. Nevertheless, an ad hoc Intergovernmental Working Group on the Problem of Corrupt Practices, which was set up by ECOSOC Resolution 2041, held it first meeting in November 1976. This and subsequent meetings were attended by a large number of developing and Western industrialized countries. During the second session in early 1978, the United States submitted another working paper which contained similar ideas to those presented to ECOSOC in the fall of 1976 , as outlined in the preceding pages. (2) The thrust of the United States effort was the obligation by each signatory of the agreement to ensure that its criminal laws prohibiting bribery of its public officials would apply to international commercial transactions and related official acts as defined in the agreement. All signatories would endeavor to prosecute both those who offer or give bribes and those who demand, solicit, or receive bribes.

While some delegations fully agreed with the United States proposal and considered it a sound basis for the discussion of the working group, others felt that it took too restrictive a view of the scope of corrupt practices. Some members of the Group of "77" thought that insufficient attention had been given to the issue of payment of taxes and royalties by MNCs in contravention of United Nations resolutions. (3)

After extensive discussions in subsequent sessions, and the submission of additional proposals, a general consensus emerged that the offense of bribery, both active and passive, should be criminalized in national law and that appropriate penalties should be instituted by national legislation. The term "bribe" was to be interpreted broadly, but there was disagreement as to whether the act of bribery had to be simply in connection with an international commercial transaction, or whether it was being carried out for the specific purpose of obtaining or retaining such a transaction.

Another problem discussed at length was the extension of jurisdiction beyond the territory of the state that had passed legislation to criminalize illicit payments. If the nationality principle is accepted, a state can prosecute one of its nationals wherever he might   have committed the offense. Under the territoriality principle, the offender can be prosecuted only if the act was committed within the state's borders.   For states operating under this principle, a so-called "territorial link" has to be introduced between the   offense and the territory of the state of which the offender is a national if he committed the bribery outside his own country. This was the solution chosen by the United States in the Foreign Corrupt Practices Act passed in December 1977. (4)

Other legal questions have also prevented a successful conclusion of the working group's efforts so far. Nevertheless, the prospects for the elaboration of an international draft agreement seem to be fairly good if a sincere will exists on the part of the delegations to reach a consensus on the various legal points that have been raised, and if these points are not used as a pretext to scuttle the whole undertaking for self-serving reasons. In the meantime, the approprite provisions of the code of conduct on abstention from corrupt practices, which should be linked with the results of the more specialized working group although the code's scope is much narrower, cannot be formulated until the outcome of the group's deliberations is known.

THE TRANSFER OF TECHNOLOGY

Perhaps nothing has more disturbed and upset Third World leaders than the lack of technology and scientific know-how in their countries. They perceive the full possessors of such know-how to be the superpowers and the rich countries. Thus, it is not surprising that they want to change the rules of the game regarding technological and industrial property rights in accordance with the principles of the NIEO and the Charter of Economic Rights and Duties of States.   UNCTAD has been and continues to be the logical forum for these efforts.

The efforts of   UNCTAD in developing a code of conduct on the transfer of technology have progressed further than those on the code for MNCs in general. Draft outlines of the former were formulated early in 1975 by Brazil for the Group of "77" and by Japan for the Western industrialized countries. Their documents were circulated for the UNCTAD Trade and Development Board meeting in May of that year, and then expanded and revised in November 1975. (5)

The framework of the UNCTAD efforts can be seen best by quoting from item 12 of the Provisional Agenda for the Fourth Session of UNCTAD in Nairobi in May 1976:

> [A] new phase is beginning in the developing countries-- a phase marked by a radical shift of vision and the search for new policies. The peripheral policies of the past, involving minor modification to existing forms of relationships, are being replaced by a search for fresh patterns drawing upon economic, social, and cultural resources indigenous to the territories of the Third World. The strengthening of national technological capabilities is assuming a central place in development plans and policies. Attempts are therefore being made progressively to loosen those ties with developed countries which hamper the attainment of this objective, and to move towards greater co-operation among countries themselves. (6)

UNCTAD's concern with the need for altering the existing international legal environment and practices in the area of technology transfer to meet the interests and perceived needs of the Third World dates back to the first UNCTAD Conference in 1964. However, despite some major studies undertaken by the UNCTAD Secretariat and the formulation of action programs for the governments of LDCs (including regional and interregional cooperation as well as action by advanced countries), little was done between 1972 and 1975 to implement these plans. In May 1975 an Integovernmental Group of Experts on the Code of Conduct on Transfer of Technology, which was convened by the secretary of UNCTAD, considered the two earlier-mentioned separate draft outlines on the subject matter. To push this endeavor along, resolution 3362, adopted during the Seventh Special Session of the General Assembly of the United Nations, stated:

> All States should co-operate in evolving an international code of conduct for the transfer of technology, corresponding, in particular, to the special needs of the developing countries. Work on such a code should therefore be continued within the United Nations Conference on Trade and Development and concluded in time for decisions to be reached at the fourth session of the Conference, including a decision on the legal character of such a code with objective of the adoption of a code of conduct prior to the end of 1977. . . .

Although this deadline has not been met, considerable progress has been made, as we will see later. Meanwhile, as a collateral endeavor to the code on technology transfer, UNCTAD has also embarked on efforts to restructure the existing industrial property systems and to revise the Paris Convention for the Protection of Industrial Property of 1883 as amended. These efforts were guided by a number of considerations, of which the following seem to be most significant:

1. The importation of the patented product is not as a general rule a substitute for the working of the patent in the developing country granting it

2. More adequate provisions are required to avoid abuses of patent rights and to increase the probability of patents being worked in the developing country granting them.

3. The introduction of forms of protection of inventions other than traditional patents (e.g., inventor's certificates, industrial development patents, and technology transfer patents) should be examined.

4. The need for technical assistance to developing countries in the field of industrial property, and in particular for expanded access to and utilization of patent documentation by developing countries must be recognized, in order to facilitate the transfer, absorption, adaptation and creation of suitable technology

5. An in-depth review of the provisions on trade marks should be carried out

6. There should be new ad imaginative studies of possibilities of giving preferential treatment to all developing countries.... (7)

In order to make the efforts for a code on technology transfer and for review of the patent laws meaningful for most LDCs, UNCTAD has also recognized the need for requisite institutional machinery. Technical personnel must be trained and perhaps exchanged, regional joint research centers may be useful, and information centers have to be set up that can also handle the dissemination and exchange of technologies originating in developing countries. But again, while the ideas are there, they must be translated into reality. Rapid industrialization aided by new patent and technology transfer systems may seem to be a very meritorious goal in the minds of LDC government leaders, but without a proper infrastructure it may be nothing but a pleasant vista of the future, regardless of the economic and political philosophies of many of thes leaders.

The Group of "77" Code Draft Outline

These philosophical tendencies were reflected in the draft of the code presented by the Group of "77", which minces no words about its intentions, especially in its preamble. Technology is seen as "a part of universal human heritage to which all countries have the 'right' of access in order to improve the living standards of their people. All countries have therefore the 'duty' to promote the transfer of technology, whether proprietary or otherwise, on favorable terms" in accordance with the national policies, plans, and priorities of the developing countries. Indeed, an adequate transfer should become an "effective instrument for the elimination of economic inequality among countries and for the establishment of a new and more just international economic order." For this reason, the code should be "universally applicable" and legally binding internationally. (8)

Of course, preambles tend to be hyperbolic, and in the body of the proposed code the tone is less strident. Emphasis is placed on the obvious right of home and host countries to regulate the transfer of technology through national legislation. Such legislation must assure protection of domestic recipient enterprises and prevent in genera the displacement of national enterprises by foreign collaboration arrangements. Payments for technology are to be treated as profit whenever such payments are made to parent companies or other subsidiaries of an MNC or the supplier and recipient companies "form economic unit or have community of interests."

A long chapter of the proposed draft outline deals with restrictive business practices in the transfer of technology. Forty-odd specific restrictions are enumerated that are seen as possibly having an adverse effect on the technology recipient. Some of these restrictions, such as the prohibition of horizontal cartel activities, are reasonable and should be supportable by MNCs and their home country governments; others are likely to be rejected as unduly limiting the freedom of contractual agreements between supplier firms and recipient enterprises.

Another chapter requires numerous guarantees from enterprises supplying technology. Apart from assurances that the technology will perform as stipulated, the guarantees include adequate training of nationals in the use of the technology received and fair pricing for needed materials imported and goods produced when they can be sold only to the technology supplier or any other enterprises designated by him. Priorities must be given to the employment of local research and development skills and experience and to the full use of technology already available in the recipient country.

In addition to the strong bias in favor of technology recipients evident in the draft proposal, special preferential treatment is stipulated for enterprises in developing countries. This includes fiscal and other special incentives for technology suppliers in the developed countries to induce them to provide the most favorable conditions to the Third World countries for the technology transfer and use and the assurance by the supplier countries not to restrict imports of products from developing countries that have been manufactured by means of the newly acquired technologies. Assistance is also to be given by the governments of developed supplier countries for the establishments of national, regional, and international institutions that can help the Third World in their quest for obtaining greater technological capabilities.

For the settlement of disputes arising from technology transfer agreements, the laws of the technology-receiving country are to apply. Only if these laws specifically permit recourse to arbitration in this field can the parties concerned submit such disputes to arbitration in accordance with procedures which they have agreed.

Proposals of the Western Industrialized Countries

A wide conceptual gap separated the Group of "77" draft outline from the initial proposal of the industrially advanced countries, which insisted on voluntary compliance by MNCs and governments and on maximum freedom and the sanctity of contractual agreements. The bial of this proposal was clearly in favor on MNCs and the"proper" investment climate, although the basic needs of Third World countries for appropriate technology were acknowledged and the legitimacy of some of their demands were recognized. The problem of restrictive business practices is dealt with in one line and the responsibilities of technology-supplying enterprises and their governments are couched in qualifying terms such as "to the extent practicable," "feasible," "appropriate," and "reasonable."

The revised draft outline on technology transfer submitted by the Western industrialized countries in November 1975 was much more comprehensive and positive, thereby narrowing the gap appreciably between the Third World and the Western industrialized camps. Of course, the insistence on the voluntary nature of the code of conduct has remained, and respect for individual agreements under international law continues to be stressed. Perhaps reflecting the changed United States foreign policy that manifested itself during the Seventh Special Session of the United Nations General Assembly in September 1975 and the apparent, though qualified, responsiveness of the Third World leadership to American policy suggestions, the revised proposal clearly stated that the development of indigenous technological capabilities in the Third World should be promoted, and that restrictive business practices adversely affecting the transfer of technology should be avoided. Moreover, details for the implementation of these objectives were stipulated by assigning specific responsibilities to technology source and recipient enterprises and governments. As a result, accommodations have been made to some of the demands made on MNCs in the Group of "77" outline, although the concessions on restrictive business practices fell far short of meeting the concepts of some members of the Group of "77" according to which any action by technology suppliers is objectionable that might limit accessiblity to technological know-how or otherwise place recipient countries in positions of some kind of hardship. (9) Nevertheless, the eight restrictive business practices that were listed in the Western group's proposal are highly important and include:

1. Restrictions in patent or know-how licenses that unreasonably prevent the export of unpatented products or components, or which unreasonably restrict export to countries where the product made pursuant to the licensed technology is not patented

2. Provisions having the effect of causing tied sales, i.e., which oblige or impel the licensee to accept unwanted and unneeded licenses, or purchase unwanted and unneeded goods or services from the licenser or his designated source

3. Restrictions preventing the exploitation of a licensed process or product after the date of expiry of a patent under which the license is granted, or requiring royalties to be paid for the use of these patents as such after that date

4. Requiring the licensee to assign or grant back to the licensor exclusively all improvements discovered in working the subject matter of the license, when the effect of this practice is to abuse a dominant position of the licensor. (10)

Of course, the revised proposal of the Western group continued to emphasize the confidentiality and proprietary nature of trade secrets and know-how acquired in connection with the transfer of technology. It opposed the view that the law of the recipient state should determine which legal rules should apply for settlement of disputes arising from the transfer of technology and wanted the parties to pertinent agreements to choose freely the applicable law, including arbitration.

Despite the narrowing of the disparities between the draft outlines, by the end of 1975 considerable differences continued to exist prior to the Nairobi meeting of UNCTAD. Howard V. Perlmutter and Taghi Saghafi-nejad worked up a concise and penetrating comparison between the positions of the two groups on the code which is found in slightly modified form in table 6.1. Although this table is generally self-explanatory, a few comments will serve to summarize the preceding discussion. For the Group of "77", access to technology is regarded almost as a "natural" right, and technology as a public good, while the Western industrialized countries insist on technology falling essentially into the category of private property with all the implications that flow from that notion.

An important difference is the demand of the Group of "77" that the code be legally binding. We can see here an analogy to the civil rights movement in the United States which fought hard and successfully to ensure that their demands be backed up by appropriate changes in the law, either through Supreme Court decisions or Federal legislation. It seems that Third World leaders feel that once the law is on their side, the battle for unfettered access will be won. Whether reality will vindicate this expectation is not entirely sure. It involves training personnel by recipient countries to screen technology and to use it, which is a long-term process. Technological dependence may not be eliminated except over periods counted more in decades than in years, especially since the economic posture of LDCs shows wide variance with many small countries having only very limited markets and very poor personnel resources.

Interesting differences can also be found in the last three issues in table 6.1. The Group of "77" makes little mention of the duties of the recipient countries, emphasizing the notion of sovereignty in LDCs dealing with MNCs. Thus, for these countries the legal obligations apply mostly to the technology-supplying firms and the code reduces their control over the transfer process. This orientation is also visible in the settlement of disputes to be carried out through the laws of the

TABLE 6.1. Comparison of the Group of "77" and Western Advanced Group Positions on Codes of Conduct for Transfer of Technology

Issue	Group of "77"	Western Advanced Group	Synthesis
Nature of technology (T)	T is part of universal human heritage, all countries have the right of access to it.	T is developed using primarily private resources.	Fundamental ideological and philosophical difference, but Western group stops short of calling T completely private.
Transfer of technology (T.T.)	Should become an effective instrument for elimination of inequality among countries, promotes NIEO.	Should be encouraged, all parties should abide by equitable general rules, and should be aware of conditions; each T.T. is unique.	T.T. as a vehicle for development, vs. uniqueness and equitable general rules.
Code's legal status	An international legally binding code.	A nonbinding code of general and voluntary nature.	Main obstacle was to be resolved in 1976 (Nairobi) but no agreement by end of 1979.
Restrictive business practices (RBP)	Consists of 40 items.	May '75: only touched upon; Nov. '75: a whole section with 8 separate items.	Definitions different. When RBPs mentioned by Western Group position falls short of "77"s position and definitions.
Obligations	Primarily fall on supplying firms. Little mention of duties of recipient countries.	Fall on suppliers, recipient states to carry out part of responsibilities.	States are sovereign to "77" and just one of several parties to Western Group.
Dispute settlement	Through laws and courts of recipient country, if these nonexistent, then according to each contractural agreement.	Parties to a T.T. agreement to be permitted to freely choose and specify in contract.	Western Group wants international law to dominate in arbitration. "77" won't jeopardize sovereignty.

Source: Howard V. Perlmutter and Taghi Saghafi-nejad, "Process or Product? A Social Architectural Perspective of Codes of Conduct to Technical Transfer and Development." Prepared for presentation at the International Studies Association 1976 Convention, Toronto, Canada, February 18, 1976, p. 17.

recipient countries.   On the other hand, the Western groups want international law to predominate so that they may rely on arbitration, if so as specified in transfer agreements.

Despite these differences, the West and, in particular, the United States seems to gradually embrace more of the LDC position.   In September 1975, Secretary of State Henry Kissinger, addressing the Seventh Special Session of the United Nations General Assembly, stated:

> The United States is prepared to meet the proper concerns of governments in whose territories transnational enterprises operate. We affirm that enterprises must act in full accordance with the sovereignty of host governments and take full account of their public policy.   Countries are entitled to regulate the operations of transnational enterprises within their borders, but countries wishing the benefits of these enterprises should foster the conditions that attract and maintain their productive operation.

> The United States therefore believes that the time has come for the international community to articulate standards of conduct for both enterprises and governments. (11)

The UNCTAD Conference in Nairobi

It would have been unrealistic to hope that as unwieldy a conference as any of the UNCTAD quadrennial general meetings could bridge the gaps existing between the approaches to the transfer of technology taken by the Western industrialized countries and the Third World. Nevertheless, progress toward the elaboration of a code of conduct was made, although this progress was mainly procedural rather than substantive. The major decision was to establish within UNCTAD an Intergovernmental Group of Experts on the Code of Conduct on the Transfer of Technology open to participation by member states in order to work up a draft of the code.   This Group of Experts was to be free to formulate draft provisions ranging from mandatory to optional and voluntary "without prejudice to the final decision on the legal character of the code of conduct." (12)   That decision was postponed to a special United Nations conference to be convened by the General Assembly.   Held in the fall of 1978, this conference was to negotiate the final draft of the code of conduct on the transfer of technology and make the necessary decisions for its adoption.   However, it did not succeed fully, and another conference with this purpose had to be held in the spring of 1979.

The Nairobi meeting also addressed itself to creating the necessary infrastructure for the development, transfer, and use of technology in the Third World.   To this end, it adopted a long list of recommendations, some of which paralleled the measures suggested in the revised draft outline for the code submitted by the Western industrialized countries. For the developing countries, the recommendations included the formulation of a technology plan as part of their national development plans, the establishment of appropriate institutional machinery in the form of a national center for the development and transfer of technology, and optimum utilization of qualified manpower resources. Major emphasis was placed on cooperation among Third World countries by preferential technology arrangements among themselves and the creation of subregional, regional, and interregional centers that could serve as essential links with the national centers. There was, of course, also a long list of actions and measures recommended for the developed countries that was likely to contribute to the successful transfer and use of technology by Third World countries and to the expansion of their capacities to develop technology on their own, including the establishment of a United Nations University. (13)

Much of what has been recommended by UNCTAD IV in Nairobi with respect to technology transfer had become American foreign policy prior to the conference. In his speech at the opening session of the conference, Secretary of State Kissinger declared:

> First, to adapt technology to the needs of developing countries, the United States supports the establishment of a network of research and development institutions at the local, regional, and international levels. We need to strengthen global research capacities for development and to expand intergovernmental cooperation ....
>
> The second element of our program is to improve the amount and quality of technological information available to developing countries and to improve their selection of technology relevant to their needs.... For its part, the United States will inventory its national technological information resources and make available .... consultants and other services to improve access to our National Library of Medicine, the Division of Scientific Information of the National Science Foundation, the National Agricultural Library, and the Smithsonian Information Service...
>
> Third, to nurture new generations of technologists and technology managers, the United States proposes a priority effort to train individuals who can develop, identify, and apply technology suited to the needs of developing countries....
>
> The fourth element of our approach is to make the process of transferring existing technology more effective and equitable....

The United States also supported the creation of an UNCTAD Advisory Service to strengthen the ability of Third World countries to identify, select, and negotiate for the technology most appropriate to their requirements. The Nairobi Conference decided to set up such an organization from the regular budget of UNCTAD. (15) Another project adopted by the Conference and supported by the United States was the convening of a United Nations Conference on Science and Technology Development in 1979. (16) Finally, it was decided that UNCTAD should continue to play an important role in the reappraisal of the international patent system and, in particular, in the revision of the Paris Convention for the Protection of Industrial Property as it affects the transfer of technology to the developing countries. (17) However, the United States proposal for a multi-billion dollar International Resources Bank that could assist the Third World in obtaining needed technology was rejected by the conference. The likely reason for the rejection was the private-investor orientation of the proposed bank, under which the funds of the bank would be used by private corporations for natural resources developments and at the same time aid in the improvement of technological, managerial, and marketing capabilities in the host country. Again, the bias against private enterprise and concomitant fear of outside domination, so frequently found in Third World motivation, appeared to carry the day.

The Technology Transfer Draft Code

Perhaps somewhat aided by the United States government's more favorable stance toward LDC demands regarding technology, as well as by the Working Group of Experts and the two United Nations conferences on this subject, progress toward an agreed text of a code was made. The code consists of the following parts: a preamble; definitions and scope of application; objectives and principles; national regulation of transfer of technology transactions; restrictive practices involving the transfer of technology; responsibilities and obligations of parties; special treatment for developing countries and international collaboration; and applicable law and settlement of disputes. The scope is broad, and its coverage includes patented and unpatented technology, turn-key agreements, and leasing of machinery. It applies only to the international transfer of technology, but covers a variety of enterprises and governments, and its application goes beyond MNCs. Indeed, parties to a technology transfer may be

> any person, both natural and juridical, of public or private law either individual or collective, including corporations, companies, partnerships and other associations and organizations, whether owned, controlled or created by individuals, juridical persons, Governments...or any combination thereof, when it engages in international transfer of technology.... The term also applies to States, Government agencies and international ...organizations when they engage in international transfer of technology transactions. (18)

The inclusion of state-owned entities and, therefore, state-owned MNCs is noteworthy because the working group on the MNC code of conduct has not arrived at a decision in this matter. Another point needs to be emphasized: it has been agreed that the technology-transfer code will apply to intracorporate transactions, provided that the transfer passes national boundaries. (19)

It is significant that major agreement has been reached on the objectives of the technology transfer code. They include:

(i) To establish general and equitable standards which should form... a basis of the relationships among parties to transfer of technology transactions..., taking into consideration their legitimate interests, and giving due recognition to the special needs of developing countries for the fulfillment of their economic and social development objectives....

(ii) To encourage transfer of technology transactions, particularly those involving developing countries, under conditions where bargaining positions of the parties to the transactions are balanced in such a way as to avoid abuses of a stronger position and thereby to achieve mutually satisfactory agreements.

(iii) To facilitate and increase the international flow of technological information, particularly on the availability of alternative technologies as a prerequisite for the assessment, selection, adaptation, development, and use of technologies in all countries, particularly in developing countries.

(iv) To facilitate and increase the international flow of proprietary and nonproprietary technology for strengthening the growth of the scientific and technological capabilities of all countries, in particular developing countries, so as to increase their participation in world production and trade.

(v) To increase the contributions of technology to the identification and solution of social and economic problems of all countries, particularly the developing countries, including the development of basic sectors of their national economies.

(vi) To facilitate the formulation, adoption, and implementation of national policies, laws, and regulations on the subject of transfer of technology by setting forth international norms. (UN ECOSOC Document E/C.10/AC.2/5 July 18, 1978,p.8.)

We have observed in table 6.1 that the draft proposals by the Group of "77" and the Western group on restrictive practices in 1976 were still far apart, although some rapprochement could be discerned. By 1979, further substantial progress was made: The Group of "77" had lowered its list of restrictive practices from 40 to 20, and the Western group had expanded its list from eight to 16. In fact, some of the provisions now have an agreed text and in quite a few others the wording is relatively close, a major difference being the inclusion of qualifying words such as "unreasonable" in the Western proposal. (20)   Some progress on the substance has also been made on the obligations of the parties to technology transfers, (21) but any kind of agreement remains elusive with respect to the code's legal nature.

Which provisions of the much more comprehensive technology-transfer code will find their way into the MNC code of conduct is difficult to predict. Obviously, only those directly relevant to the operations of MNCs will be considered, and they concern restrictive practices and details of the transfer of technology. However, provisions dealing with transfer pricing, consumer protection, and special treatment for LDCs of both codes may have to be reconciled, since differences in the exact wording of these provisions may raise problems as to their intended effect.

RESTRICTIVE BUSINESS PRACTICES

In 1976, UNCTAD IV established the Ad Hoc Group of Experts on Restrictive Business Practices, the main mission of which is to formulate

> a set of multilaterally agreed equitable principles and rules for the control of restrictive business practices having adverse effects on international trade, particularly that of developing countries, and on the economic development of these countries. (22)

This mandate has been interpreted by the group as envisaging a series of coherent and mutually supporting measures, basically of two kinds: principles and rules to govern the use of restrictive business practices by enterprises, including multinational corporations; and principles for control of action by governments at national, regional, and international levels.

In agreed text of the group's members, restrictive business practices are defined as

> acts or behaviour of enterprises which, through an abuse or acquisition and abuse of a dominant position of market power, limit access to markets or otherwise unduly restrain competition, having or being likely to have adverse effects on international trade, particularly that of developing countries, and on the economic development of these countries, or which through formal, informal, written or unwritten agreements or arrangements among enterprises have the same effects. (23)

There is no requirement that the restrictive business practices to be covered by the code take place in more than one country; that is to say, that the practices concerned be international in character. The agreed text explicitly provides that the code's principles and rules apply irrespective of whether such practices involve enterprises in one or more countries. The impact of the practices in question may be international - to the extent that international trade is involved - but may also be solely domestic in character where the economic development of a developing country is affected.

The subjects of the code on restrictive business practices of course include MNCs, but also encompass many other entities. In the agreed text, the subjects are "enterprises," which means firms, partnerships, corporations, companies, other associations, natural or juridical persons, or any combination thereof, whether created or controlled by States, legal entities or individuals, which are engaged in commercial activities, and includes their branches, subsidiaries, affiliates, or other entities directly or indirectly controlled by them.... (24)

Moreover, the code covers foreign and foreign-owned enterprises as well as domestic ones.

Agreed specifics regarding the details of restrictive business practices and the treatment of various enterprises are still scanty. One of the proposed texts presented by the Group of "77" provides that developing countries may exempt in their legislation and regulations certain industries, enterprises, acts, agreements, etc. that are essential for their economic development or for defense of their primary commodities and economic resources. As a consequence:

In the implementation of the multilaterally agreed equitable principles and rules, account should be taken of the economic conditions in developing countries and the frequent absence of countervailing market power of enterprises of those countries to that of enterprises of developed countries, especially transnational corporations, and accordingly preferential or differential treatment should be afforded to their national enterprises in order to ensure the equitable application of the principles and rules. (25)

Whether this strong tilt toward Third World is acceptable to the Western group is doubtful, since nondiscriminatory treatment remains an important principle on the part of the Western industrialized countries, despite a more sympathetic ear lent to Third World claims. So far, they are also reluctant to accept another proposal in which MNCs shall

refrain from using their market power over the supply of goods and services as a means of acquiring ownership or control of national enterprises in developing countries; and refrain from establishing with other transnational corporations joint ventures in developed and developing countries, the results of which are likely to foreclose those markets to any effective domestic competition, including imports in particular from developing countries. (26)

Perhaps some compromises can be found; in his speech in 1975 to the Special Session of the United Nations General Assembly, Henry Kissinger seemed to open the door, however slightly, to LDC concerns regarding restrictive business practices when he said:

Laws against restrictive business practices must be developed, better coordinated among countries, and enforced. The United States has long been vigilant against such abuses in domestic trade, mergers, or licensing of technology. We stand by the same principles internationally.   We condemn restrictive practices in setting prices or restraining supplies, whether by private or stateowned transnational enterprises or by the collusion of national governments. (27)

Another crucial question remains in the deliberation of this code as well as for the other codes: its legal nature.   Some countries would like the states to implement the code's provisions in their national laws, while others would like to see compliance with the code to be entirely voluntary.   Thus, the Working Group on the Code of Conduct on MNCs will be faced not only with the problem of selecting particular provisions from the restrictive business practices endeavor for its own instrument, but also with the pervasive dilemma regarding its scope and legal nature.

EMPLOYMENT AND LABOR: THE ILO DECLARATION

Work in the ILO regarding MNCs was initiated in 1971.   As the views differed considerably between the workers' and employees' represenatives on the impact of MNCs on social policy, the director-general of the ILO was requested "to undertake a study on the usefulness of international principles and guidelines in the field of social policy relating to the activities of multinational enterprises and the elements and implications of such principles and guidelines." (28)

The significance of this study is illustrated by the fact that MNCs directly employ between 13 and 14 million people in the market-economy countries.   This total does not take into account the indirect effects on employment or of jobs created through the activities of MNCs other than by direct investment. (29)   Moreover, the effect on employment varies enormously from sector to sector and country to country.   As production and economic patterns changed in the developed countries as the result of   MNC operations, more workers were employed in some industries, while substantial jobs were lost in others, the textile industry being a prime example of the latter.   In some of the LDCs, such as Brazil, Mexico, and Taiwan, sometimes called the New Industrial Countries (NICS), MNC investment has helped employment considerably.   In others, the effects have been negligible.

It was obvious, then, that the ILO study would not only be useful, but, in fact, very much needed.   In 1976, a Tripartite Advisory Meeting considered the ILO study and recommended that work be initiated on an ILO Tripartite Declaration of Principles Concerning Multinational Enterprises and Social Policy.   This declaration was seen to be nonmandatory in character to be effective for all MNCs (whether of public, mixed, or private ownership) and to take account of the sovereign rights of states.   The declaration seemed to give due consideration to the relevant national laws and practices and to accepted international obligations while referring to ILO conventions and recommendations for guidance in employment policies.

The meeting recommended that the tripartite declaration, once approved by the governing body, should, if appropriate, be officially transmitted to the United Nations for incorporation in the proposed code of conduct drafted by the Commission on Transnational Corporations. Participants of the meeting felt that in doing so, it should be made clear that the tripartite declaration had been devised as a document of voluntary character and should be recognized as such without prejudice to the legal character of the United Nations code of conduct.

In order to prepare a draft text, a small tripartite group was established, which upon completion of its work submitted the draft text to a reconvened Tripartite Advisory Meeting. (30) After that, the draft text was submitted to the governing body which adopted it in November 1977 and transmitted it to the United Nations with a view to incorporate it, as appropriate, in the code of conduct for MNCs. (31)

A brief summary of the contents of the declaration is instructive. (32) Its expressed goal is to encourage the positive contribution that MNCs can make to economic and social progress and to minimize and resolve the difficulties that their operations may cause. It pays special attention to the United Nations resolutions advocating a new international economic order.

The declaration admonishes MNCs to consider carefully the established policy objectives of their host countries and keep their activities in harmony with the development priorities and social aims of these countries. To this end, consultations should be held between MNCs, the governments, and, wherever appropriate, national employers' and workers' organizations. Governments of home countries should promote good social practice among their MNCs, urging them to uphold social and labor laws in host countries and to comply with relevant international standards.

With respect to employment, the declaration calls for stimulating economic growth and development, raising living standards, meeting manpower requirements, and overcoming unemployment and under-employment. MNCs, particularly when operating in developing countries, should endeavour to increase employment opportunities and standards. When investing in developing countries, MNCs should try to use technologies that generate employment both directly and indirectly. All governments should pursue policies designed to promote equality of opportunity and treatment in employment, seek to eliminate any discrimination based on race, color, sex, religion, political opinion, nationality, or social origin. MNCs should make qualifications, skill, and experience the bases for the recruitment, placement, training, and advancement of their staff at all levels. In view of the flexibility that multinational enterprises may have, they should strive to assume a leading role in promoting security of employment.

MNCs should ensure that training is provided for their employees to meet the needs of the host countries enterprise and national development policies. This responsibility should be carried out, where appropriate, in cooperation with the authorities of the country and with employers' and workers' organizations.

Conditions of work in MNC entities and wages and benefits should not be less favorable than those offered by comparable local employers. In developing countries, where comparable employers may not exist, MNCs should provide the best possible wages, benefits, and conditions of work, which should at least satisfy the basic needs of the workers and their families. MNCs should maintain the highest standards of safety and health in conformity with national requirements, bearing in mind their own experience in the field and knowledge of special hazards.

In the field of industrial relations, MNCs should maintain standards at least as good as those observed by comparable employers in the country where they operate. Workers employed by multinational as well as national enterprises should, without exception, have the right to establish and join organizations of their own choosing without previous authorization, and be protected against antiunion discrimination. Moreover, MNCs should provide workers' representatives with information required for meaningful negotiations in accordance with local law and practices.

On the other side, governments of host countries should not attempt to attract foreign investment by limiting workers freedom of association or right to organize and bargain collectively. Worker representatives in MNCs should not be prevented from meeting to consult and exchange views, so long as this does not adversely affect the functioning of the enterprise and relationships with representative organizations of their own choosing, recognized for the purpose of collective bargaining.

MNCs should not threaten to transfer an operating unit or section from the country in order to influence bona fide negotiations with workers' representatives on conditions of employment or impede the exercise of workers' rights to organize.

It is quite evident that the declaration is a balanced instrument that recognizes the particular needs of the LDCS while respecting the legitimate requirements of a viable business enterprise. This was recognized by the International Organization of Employees in a lengthy statement to the seventh session of the working group in March 1979. (33) Hence, it was not difficult for the working group on the code of conduct to reach agreement to make a reference to the tripartite declaration in the provisions on employment and labor in both chapter 3, "Activities of Transnational Corporations" and to repeat this reference as far as governments are concerned in chapter 4 "Treatment of Transnational Corporation." The tentative text in chapter 3 reads as follows:

B. Employment and Labour

Transnational corporations should adhere to the principles in the field of

(a) Employment, and in particular in respect to employment promotion, equality of opportunity, and treatment and security of employment;

(b) Training;

(c) Conditions of work and life, and in particular in respect to wages, benefits, conditions of work, and safety and health;

(d) Industrial relations, and in particular in respect to freedom of association and the right to organize, collective bargaining, consultation, examination of grievances, and settlement of industrial disputes.

set out in the Tripartite Declaration of Principles concerning Multinational Enterprises and Social Policy, adopted by the Governing Body of The International Labour Office.

In addition, the working group on the code of conduct has considered a tentative formulation regarding disclosure of information by MNCs to trade unions for inclusion in the code. This formulation which is agreeable to the members of the group states:

> Transnational corporations should provide to trade unions or other representatives of employees, information on their structure, activities, and policies, and other matters dealt with in the Code which would be necessary to obtain an accurate view of the performance of the entity, or, where appropriate, the enterprise as a whole, and necessary to represent the legitimate interests of the employees of the transnational corporation concerned.   Such information should include, in accordance with national laws, regulations and practices, future plans and policy options having major economic and social consequences on employees. (34)

Clearly, the ILO tripartite declaration is the success story of the endeavor to draft the code of conduct. But does it augur well for the difficult problem of the legal nature of the code and its implementation? We will examine these issues in the next chapter.

7 Definitions, Legal Nature, and Implementation

WHAT KIND OF MNC?

The problem of definitions has plagued the work on the code since the Group of Eminent Persons was involved in preparing its report. As was mentioned in chapter 3, the question of definition affects the applicability of the prospective code and is, therefore, highly significant.

The Commission on Transnational Corporations took up the question of definition during its first session. Some delegations expressed the view that the definition should be broad enough to cover direct international investment activities by state-owned companies, and thus supported the definition used in the report of the Group of Eminent Persons. Several delegations (communist countries) maintained that state-owned enterprises should be excluded as not being geared mainly to profit making and that the term "transnational corporations" referred only to private enterprises. In 1977, the German Democratic Republic asserted that its foreign-trade organizations and their affiliates "can in no way be regarded as, or put on one level with, transnational corporations." (1)

Although the definitional issue became part of the commission's program and was discussed in all sessions, no decision could be reached. The United States, as mentioned earlier, insisted on the inclusion of state-owned enterprises even if their activities were not geared to profit making, and most Western delegations shared this view. Others - especially the communist delegations - objected, probably because it would subject these state-owned and operated entities to the control of the code, adversely affecting the sovereignty principle so important to these countries. For tactical reasons, LDCs have supported this position, largely because this would assure them the backing of the communist countries for their proposals and views.

It is interesting to note that this problem of definition did not create major difficulties in the work on the code regarding technology transfer and corrupt practices nor on the ILO Declaration. In other forums, various definitions of MNCs were used, and these were related closely to the purpose at hand. For example, the Group of Experts on International Standards of Accounting and Reporting defines corporation by size criteria in order not to overburden smaller entities with its comprehensive recommendations. On the other hand, national laws of host countries regarding the activities of MNCs often give no size limits, or if they do, they may vary with the size of the country. The 1973 guidelines of the European Economic Community state that a "multinational undertaking...is an undertaking with production facilities in at least two countries"; (2) it refrains from further quantitative criteria because they tend to be arbitrary and imprecise. (3) Finally, the OECD Guidelines for Multinational Enterprises, to be discussed in the next chapter, consider a precise legal definition to be completely unnecessary. This may be wise, because a number of criteria may make a particular corporation qualify at a given point of time, but fail to do so at another.

Indeed, the term "corporation" in the context of the code should not be taken to convey a particular legal form. Individual "corporations" with multiple affiliates in different countries and border crossing links may be owned by individuals or a family. For example, the Robert Bosch Company, a well-known automotive ignition firm, is family owned. In turn, foreign-based affiliates may be branches or locally incorporated subsidiaries, and these affiliates can be tied together in very complex chains of ownership.

Finally, control of a foreign subsidiary does not necessarily mean that the MNC owns all or even a majority of stock. In many instances, a minority holding, sometimes very small, is sufficient to exercise control. Moreover, nonequity forms of conducting business have become more and more popular, and in these cases it is especially difficult to determine effective control. Management contracts in cases of nationalization, long-term purchasing agreements regarding stock, as well as licensing and franchising agreements fall into this category.

It is obvious, then, that the number of possible criteria is extensive, making the definition problem highly complex. Conflicting political considerations and interests compound this issue further. This became quite clear in the lenghty discussion in the March Intergovernmental Working Group session. Several delegations stressed the importance of making progress on this significant issue. Various quantitative and qualitative criteria for the definition of MNCs were proposed, but the question of definitional breadth and inclusion of state-owned facilities defied resolution. Therefore, the group came to the conclusion that at this stage it was impossible to reach an understanding on the difficult issue of definition. (4)

THE LEGAL NATURE

In chapter 4 we pointed to the strong commitment of the United States and other Western industrialized countries to the concept of a voluntary code that does not contain legally binding commands directed to MNC managements. The LDCs, on the other hand, continue to insist on the mandatory nature of the code as far as MNCs are concerned, while provisions directed to governments would have no binding effect.

Some Group of "77" countries have suggested a compromise under which parts of the code addressed to MNCs would be voluntary, while others would be mandatory. Moreover, it is conceivable to make distinctions regarding the legal nature of the code with respect to provisions addressed to governments. Those ensuring intergovernmental cooperation in the regulation on MNCs might be mandatory, while those dealing with various aspects of MNC treatment might be voluntary. These so-called zebra codes may offer a basis for bargaining and tradeoff in the final drafting of the code.

In this respect, determining the scope of the code may also offer various opportunities. The code could be comprehensive, covering in detail all relevant topics, or it could mainly cover principles with the elaboration of specific provisions to follow over time as MNCs and governments gain experience with the working of and compliance with the code that at the beginning would be essentially voluntary. Or the code could be only partial at the time of its initial adoption and move to progressively larger coverage later. (5)

Whichever possibility or combination of possibilities is selected will affect the time needed for negotiation and agreement on the code and its legal nature. In a partly binding and partly voluntary code, the completion of the first part is likely to take much longer than the second part. If some topics are left out or the text on those topics held only to principles, the completion may be accelerated, but the balance of the code may suffer. Finally, the commission may agree on a voluntary code composed mainly of principles, but with the goal of moving later to either a partially or fully binding instrument, as experience with the operation of the code is gained over a period of years and this experience is evaluated in triennial follow-up conferences.

What options exist to make a completed code operational? The CTC staff has elaborated six interesting modalities, which show the complexity of this process: (6)

Option A

o   The entire Code of Conduct, including provisions addressed to transnational corporations, provisions on treatment of transnational corporations, is issued in the form of a declaration contained in a resolution of the United Nations General Assembly.

o   The Code contains no provision concerning its implementation, either at the national or at the international level.

This option features a Code that is fully non-binding and voluntary.

Option B

o   The entire Code of Conduct, including provisions addressed to transnational corporations, provisions on intergovernmental co-operation, provisions on treatment of transnational corporations and provisions on implementation, is issued in the form of a declaration contained in a resolution of the United Nations General Assembly.

o   The Code includes provisions

(a) whereby the adopting States undertake to give effect to it in their national law and administrative practice, and to report regularly and on request on its application within their territory;

(b) charging a Secretariat with responsibilities concerning the collection and study of State reports on the Code's application, and preparation of studies based on such reports; and

(c) charging an international Committee with responsibility for preparing and adopting revisions of the Code.

Although under this option the code staff is voluntary, states which "adopt" it undertake to give it legal status, thereby making it, in effect, mandatory within their territories. Moreover, the Secretariat is given a monitoring role and an international committee is charged with preparing possible revisions of the code. Both of these activities are likely to encroach on the voluntary nature of the code.

Option C

o   The entire Code of Conduct, including provisions addressed to transnational corporations, provisions on intergovernmental co-operation, provisions on treatment of transnational corporations and provisions on implementation, is issued in the form of a declaration contained in a resolution of the United Nations General Assembly.

This is the same wording as for Option B, but in addition to the adopting states' undertaking and the assignment of particular functions to the Secretariat and the international committee, the following features are included:

(a)...

(b)...

(c) establishing an international Panel of independent experts serving in their personal capacity charged with the elucidation of the Code's provisions on the basis of their language and context, the interpretation of the Code on the basis of its structure and purposes, fact-finding, and other kinds of action in consultation with the parties concerned; the Panel is to act on a non-adversary, consultative basis with respect to all general and specific issues brought before it by a concerned party;

(d) charging an international Committee with responsibility for eventual revision of the Code and for recording its own concerned parties' views on the work of the Panel;

(e) providing procedures for noncompulsory settlement of disputes between the States (conciliation, arbitration and adjudication) concerning the interpretation and application of the Code.

Obviously, the tasks given the various bodies under this option make it ludicrous to continue the claim of the nonbinding nature of the code. The effect of these bodies that because of their likely composition and interests, will tend to carry out their assignments with great zeal, cannot but impose severe constraints on MNCs and make the code virtually mandatory.

Option D

o   The provisions addressed to transnational corporations are included in a Protocol (which is an international treaty, legally binding on the States adopting it).

o   The provisions on intergovernmental co-operation, the provisions on treatment of transnational corporations and the provisions on implementation are contained in a resolution of the United Nations General Assembly.

This option has all the additional features as Option C, plus an additional task for the international panel of experts to handle complaints procedures.

This option at least plainly states the mandatory nature of the code without attempting to reach the objective through the back door. Undoubtedly, this option would make MNC compliance with the code likely, but the voluntary approach to government compliance raises severe doubts regarding a balanced instrument, thereby undermining any long-range effectiveness of the code. Moreover, the promulgation of such a code would be unduly delayed and place in serious doubt the success of the whole exercise.

Option E

o   The provisions on intergovernmental co-operation and the provisions on implementation are to be included in Proctocols (i.e., international treaties).

o   The provisions addressed to transnational corporations and the provisions on treatment of transnational corporations are contained in a resolution of the United Nations General Assembly.

This option is somewhat a reversal of Option D, inasmuch as the provisions addressed to MNCs and to their treatment by governments are nonbinding, while only the provisions on intergovernmental cooperation and implementation are mandatory. Otherwise, the features listed under Option D regarding monitoring MNC activities, information collection, code interpretation, and others are the same.

At first glance, this option may be more appealing to the Western group because of the greater number of voluntary provisions. Moreover, for the LDCs and communist countries, the voluntary nature of the provisions on MNC treatment by governments may also be attractive. However, the binding force of implementation procedures and intergovernmental cooperation will shortly result in a code which de facto is more or less binding.

Option F

o   The entire Code...is in the form of an international convention;

o   The provisions addressed to transnational corporations are in an annex, which is part of the convention; adopting States undertake to enact the actual text of the annex in their national law;

o   Provisions on implementation include, as well:

(a) Undertakings by adopting States to report regularly and on request on the application of the Code within their territory;

(b) Establishment of a Secretariat, charged with collecting and studying State and transnational corporation reports on the application of the Code and preparation of studies based on such reports and on other sources;

(c) Establishment of an international Panel of independent experts charged with the elucidation of the Code, interpretation of the Code's provision on the basis of their language and context, the interpretation of the Code on the basis of its structure and purposes, fact-finding, and other kinds of action in consultation with the parties concerned; the Panel is to act on a nonadversary consultative basis, with respect to all general and specific issues brought before it by a concerned party;

(d) Charging the above-mentioned Panel with functions of complaint procedures;

(e) Charging an international committee with responsibility for eventual revision of the Code, for recording its own and other concerned parties' views on the work of the Panel and with the imposition of sanctions;

(f) Compulsory settlement of disputes procedures between States concerning the application and interpretation of the Code.

Option F offers a fully mandatory code including all phases of implementation with specific rules for complaints, code interpretation, dispute settlement with possible sanctions, and revision procedures.

While this option may be the most effective one in inducing MNCs and governments to comply with the code, in view of the comprehensiveness of the arrangements suggested, it would take decades to put the whole edifice in operation - if agreement could ever be found on the many provisions necessary under this option. It must also be kept in mind that states find themselves in such widely differing political and economic situations that acceptance of the uniformity sought by this option would be virtually impossible. In addition, placing the code's provisions into domestic law in accordance with the constitutional procedures prevailing in the 150-odd United Nations member states would take far too long and would be an almost insurmountable obstacle.

Two themes run through all six options: (a) extensive involvement of international institutions and committees in the implementation and supervisory phases of the code's functioning, and (b) an attempt to impose a degree of compliance through this institutionalized machinery, even if formally the code would be entirely nonbinding. As for the first theme, the author's anticipation of various options may well be that the CTC staff would play a major role in the code implementation and supervisory phases. This would obviously require a considerable expansion of the necessary bureaucracy to man the CTC and the new committees, a normal and understandable objective of any civil service. Since the salaries of United Nations bureaucrats are very high, it would greatly increase the United Nations budget and the cost for the member states. But while many people, especially in the Western industrialized countries, may deplore the ballooning expenses of the United Nations apparatus, (7) the second theme may be more significant and perhaps counterproductive to an early conclusion of the code negotiations. If agreement were reached on an essentially nonbinding code, it should prove itself on its own merits by voluntary adherence of MNCs and governments; and the institutional and committee structures suggested for all options in differing degrees looks like a somewhat devious way for the advocates of a binding code to achieve their aim indirectly, which proved impossible in the working group and commission negotiations. Indeed, United States State Department officials expressed their dissatisfaction to the CTC staff and other working-group delegations about the document containing the six options. Members of the State Department's Advisory Committee on International Investment, Technology, and Development stated that in their view the key element to a voluntary code was "the absence of any procedure or mechanism to judge the individual actions of a firm or reach conclusions on the alleged violations by a firm of the terms of a future code." (8)

Of course, once a code has been negotiated, some follow-up is needed to obtain a picture on the usefulness of this instrument. It would make no sense to spend millions of dollars on a large number of conferences and working-group sessions held under the auspices of the United Nations and the foreign ministries of 46 countries and then completely forget about the product of all these discussions and

negotiations.   Therefore, a follow-up procedure must be devised, and
this procedure is part of the implementation process of the code, to
which we will turn next.

IMPLEMENTATION

The formulation of a public policy or the adoption of a law or of a
"code" is not sufficient to assure that the policy or the law or the code
will be followed.   Implementation is needed, which is a process
consisting of actions providing a causal link between the goals of policy
makers, legislators, or developers of a code and the attainment of the
intended outcome.   However, implementation does not always succeed
in this task; in many cases the outcome is quite different from what was
originally intended by the originators of policies, laws, and codes.
        Regardless of whether the prospective code of conduct will be
voluntary, mandatory, or partly voluntary and partly mandatory, the
delegation of every country participating in the drafting and adopting of
the   code   must   be   expected   to   aim   at   a   degree   effectiveness.
Otherwise, participation in this long and arduous process would have
made no sense at all, or would have been pure lip service.   Undoubtedly,
even those wanting only a voluntary code see definite merit in this
enterprise, as has been shown in earlier chapters.   Nevertheless, the
degree of effectiveness will vary with the type of code adopted, and the
implementation procedures must be attuned to the type chosen.   In
particular, these procedures cannot become instruments to modify this
choice and somewhat surreptitiously introduce another, perhaps more
stringent, kind of regulation than was intended.   Yet, we should
recognize that this may well be a serious temptation for countries and
CTC staff members who would have preferred a binding code, at least
as far as MNCs are concerned.
        Having said this, let us now turn to specific aspects of code
implementation.   Some implementation tasks will have to be carried by
governments on the national level, while others will be more appro-
priately handled on the international level through intergovernmental
cooperation and international institutions.

National Level

    1. Governments must publicize the content of the code so that
governmental agencies, MNCs, labor unions, and other groups concerned
become aware of it and take it into account in their actions.   If the
code is voluntary, MNCs may be asked to announce their general
adherence in their annual report or in other company statements.

    2. Governments might express their support of a voluntary code in
official policy statements and commit themselves not to impede MNC
compliance with the code.   During the working group session in March

1979, there was general consensus regarding the importance of the application of the code at the national level.

3. Governments should take the code fully into account when introducing and implementing relevant national legislation, even if the code were to be voluntary. This concept also found broad support in the working group.

4. It may be useful to establish some kind of national body for handling matters pertaining to the code. While the basic idea was well received, the question of which particular tasks these bodies were to assume might be sensitive. Should they monitor the compliance with the code by MNCs? Or would this move a voluntary code toward the category of a mandatory code? Perhaps one of the tasks should be the resolution of difficulties relating to the application of the code which would not impair its voluntary nature. This body could also report to an international organ on the application of the code within its national boundaries.

International Level

Follow-up actions and other implementation measures on the international level are obvious for an international code, regardless of its legal nature, but their acceptability is more controversial.

1. A prime question is the selection of an existing body or the establishment of a special organ. During the working group discussion in March 1979, it was generally assumed that the Comission on Transnational Corporations, as an intergovernmental institution, would play a major role in carrying out major functions; but a few delegations thought that these functions could be exercised by a subsidiary body of the commission. However, general consensus existed that functions of a secretariat should be performed by the CTC and that in case of a binding code, any intergovernmental body that might be created should be composed of signatory states. (9)

2. The intergovernmental body should review and evaluate the application of the code on the basis of reports received from governments and, perhaps, certain nongovernmental organizations such as the International Chamber of Commerce or trade union secretariats. In this task, it should be supported by analysis of these reports by the CTC. The intergovernmental body must also serve as a forum for consultation. On both functions, the working group expressed favorable consensus.

3. A much more controversial subject, but one that needs to be addressed, is the function of the intergovernmental body to interpret and clarify the code, especially if it were voluntary. Some delegations did not want interpretation in specific cases, which would then approach the exercise of a judicial function. With respect to clarification, this function was to be strictly limited to an advisory character. MNCs and

other nongovernmental organizations such as labor unions and consumer groups should be able to present their views through their governments or directly to the intergovernmental body, as requested by this body.

4. While there will be a clear and continuing need for consultation among governments to resolve difficulties arising from the application of the code, one function for the intergovernmental body that received full approval in the working group - the possibility of assigning it functions of dispute settlement and complaints procedures - was opposed by a number of delegates. Indeed, some stated very candidly that the commission should not be entrusted with these functions and that another body should handle complaints. (10)

5. Every legal instrument may need review and revision after the passage of time. The code of conduct is no exception. Consensus emerged in the working group that such a review should be undertaken periodically, but that in order to assure legal stability after the adoption of the code, review and possible revision should not be envisaged too early. (11)

6. An important support function for proper implementation of a policy or a law is the measurement of how well the implementation process succeeds in achieving the intended policy or legal objectives. For this function the CTC's mission of collecting and disseminating information, conducting research, and preparing studies on MNCs and the application of the code is very valuable. Yet, it is also sensitive work as far as the management of MNCs is concerned, and may, at times, be resented: MNC executives may perceive the totality of information gathered and disseminated as an unwarranted, even if indirect, invasion of into their business affairs.

Intergovernmental Cooperation

To assume successful follow-up and implementation with respect to a prospective code of conduct, appropriate intergovernmental cooperation is essential. We have mentioned this topic briefly in chapter 5 when we discussed the group's chairman's formulations. The relevant provisions were found in paragraphs 57 and 58 (see appendix). These provisions were refined and expanded in a CTC Working Paper (no. 7) on February 22, 1979, which contains the common elements that have emerged in a number of tentative formulations.

The expanded provisions stress the significance of intergovernmental cooperation for enhancing the positive and reducing the negative effects of MNC activities, as well as for promoting the resolution of difficulties as a result of the application of the code. Such cooperation may take place on a bilateral, regional, and international level.

Obviously, exchange of information and consultation are crucial and are stressed in the formulations. Consultation may lead to needed agreements and arrangements on issues related to MNC activities. When negotiating such agreements concerning judicial assistance, recognition of foreign judgments, double taxation, and other such issues, the relevant provision of the order should be taken into consideration. Cooperation within the framework of regional groupings such as the European Communities and the Organization of American States to resolve common difficulties is stressed. Cooperation on a multilateral basis should make full use of the United Nations institutional machinery, particularly that concerned with the application of the code.

In the working group discussion, all delegations agreed on the importance of intergovernmental cooperation on matters related to the code, and generally were in favor of the working paper's formulations. The need of consultation was stressed in particular, and some noted the benefit of regional cooperation for increased harmonization of policies in countries of a particular region, such as Western Europe and Latin America.

SUMMARY

Despite progress on many fronts, as indicated in the last three chapters, the successful conclusion of the code negotiations must still await compromises on a number of major and minor controversies. In some of the controversies, the opposing positions on the issues are clear cut, as for example on the legal nature of the code; on others, such as how to arrive at a "balanced" code, the conflicting views may be more obscure. The precise wording of the text may also generate a number of problems. It may, therefore, be useful to take a brief look at international codes of conduct developed in other forums the OECD and the International Chamber of Commerce, (ICC) which we will proceed to in the next chapter.

8 Alternate Solutions: ICC and OECD Guidelines for MNC Conduct

The deepening concern of global public opinion and certain influential groups - especially organized labor - about some of the MNC practices and the widely heralded scenario of MNCs world being the "new sovereigns" in the world were important reasons which also induced the Organization for Economic Cooperation and Development (OECD) and the International Chamber of Commerce (ICC) to address the problem of a code of conduct. While the various United Nations bodies had struggled over a number of years to come up with an appropriate and acceptable code of conduct, the OECD and ICC were able to produce results more rapidly. The ICC, as a nongovernmental organization, had the least obstacles to overcome and adopted in December 1972 a "code" in the form of "Guidelines for International Investment", which was republished in October 1974 without change. The OECD endeavors started later, and after a year of discussion and hearings, bore fruit in June 1976 when the OECD Conference of Foreign Ministers adopted a set of "Guidelines for Multinational Enterprises." The guidelines were part of a triple effort by the OECD Committee on International Investment and Multinational Enterprises and also included an agreement on nondiscriminatory national treatment of MNC affiliates by the governments of the OECD member countries, and a cooperation arrangement on incentives and disincentives for direct international investment in OECD territories.

THE ICC GUIDELINES

We will first briefly examine the ICC guidelines because in an indirect way they contain some building stones for the OECD code. They are, of course, voluntary and require the mutual consent of MNCs and governments because, as the foreword puts it succinctly, "No government can be forced to permit foreign investment, and no investor can be forced to invest abroad on unacceptable conditions." (1)

The ICC guidelines are designed to provide starting points for MNCs and governments of both home and host countries on agreements dealing with investment policies, ownership and management problems, fiscal, commercial and labor policies, and technology. They are not a rigid code of conduct, but a set of practical recommendations based upon experience intended to promote a better understanding of the needs of the governmental and nongovernmental parties.

The basic assumption of the ICC guidelines is that private international investment is an increasingly important factor in the world economy.

> It contributes to a more effective allocation of resources and integration of markets in both industrialized and developing countries. Moreover, for a number of developing countries it is already the major external source of capital and technology and may well become increasingly important generally, in view of the relatively slow growth of official assistance. (2)

Although the guidelines generally apply to all private international direct investments, whether they originate in or are destined for developed or developing countries, some of their recommendations may be particularly relevant to an investment in the Third World. Therefore, the ICC has expressed the hope that the guidelines would find general acceptance by all countries in order to create a climate of mutual confidence that would be conducive to an increased, and mutually satisfactory, flow of international investment. As the proceedings in the various United Nations bodies have shown, these hopes have not been fulfilled.

Nevertheless, the ICC guidelines take into consideration some of the Third World demands and accommodate them as far as they can be made compatible with the basic ICC philosophy. The orientation of the guidelines reflects a mixture of enterprise and market freedom on the one hand, and definitive concerns for legitimate host country needs and policies on the other. Emphasis is placed on predictability of governmental action in both host and home country and on nondiscrimination between national firms and MNC subsidiaries.

For investment policies in general, the guidelines stress that investments should fit "satisfactorily into the economic and social development plans and priorities of the host country." At the same time, the investing MNC should inform the prospective host government of its "expectations concerning the expansion of the enterprise, employment and marketing prospects, and the financing of its operations." In turn, the host country's government should "take the fullest possible account of the need of investors for stability, continuity and growth in their operations" and refrain from discriminatory treatment on the grounds of foreign ownership, although the right to accord special treatment for any enterprise is recognized if necessary "in the interest of the economy." (3)

As for ownership and management, investing MNCs in developing countries are urged to offer, if possible, part of the equity of the subsidiary for purchase or subscription by local investors. It is not sure whether investment or participation by governmental development corporations found in many Third World countries is included in this recommendation, but clearly compulsory governmental participation is frowned upon. On the other hand, the employment and promotion of nationals to positions of increasing responsibility is urged along with relevevant training. In the event a dominant market position is abused, the guidelines, not surprisingly, advocate that the host government stimulate competition "through the encouragement of new investment and the lowering of import tariffs" rather than through "immediate application of restrictive regulations." (4)

In the field of finance, MNCs are requested to consider carefully the impact of their policies on the balance of payment of the host countries, to take into account the effects of local borrowings on the availability of funds for indigenous enterprises, and to comply with all national requirements for financial disclosure. On the other hand, host governments are asked not to place any restrictions on the remittance of payments, including profits, royalties and license fees, as well as the repatriation of capital, although it is recognized that developing countries with chronic balance of payments difficulties may require that remittances be spread over a period of time. If restrictions on the outflow of funds become necessary, the measures imposed should follow the principles of the International Monetary Fund and the General Agreement on Tariffs and Trade (GATT) and be nondiscriminatory as far as MNC subsidiaries are concerned. (5)

In the fiscal area, the main emphasis is on the avoidance of double taxation. At the same time, MNCs are exhorted to provide justification for export and import prices of their products and supplies. (6)

With respect to the treatment of foreign property, host governments are urged to respect "the recognized principles of international law," especially in the event of expropriation and nationalization when just compensation without undue delay is required. The opposition of many Third World governments to extraterritorial application of MNC home country laws and regulations interfering with the legal order of host countries is strongly supported. (7)

The section of the guidelines on labor policies accommodates an important Third World demand by urging MNCs to take into account the host government's efforts to create employment opportunities in the localities where they are most needed. Adequate advance information about the necessity of closing plants and consequent dismissals of workers is also stressed in order to minimize social damage. Home-country governments are requested to oppose restrictions on the outflow of direct investment for purposes of achieving full employment within their boundaries and instead rely on attempts to stimulate domestic demands - a set of recommendations that in some cases may fly in the face of strong domestic political pressures. (8)

In the area of technological and managerial know-how, the guidelines reflect again some of the Third World demands. They state that the investing MNE

a) Should, whenever practicable, promote the development of the technological capacity of the host country, particularly if it is a developing country, for example by the training of local staff, assistance to education institutions and, provided that conditions for efficient research so allow, by establishment in the host country of suitable research activities.

b) Should, when granted licences for the use of industrial property rights or when otherwise transferring technology, do so on reasonable terms and conditions and with an adequate market area. (9)

Moreover, the home country's government should aid developing countries in the effective use of the transferred technology by promoting appropriate scientific and educational infrastructures. Not surprisingly, there are also admonitions to the recipient country, one of which underscores the fact that technology is mainly developed by private enterprise in the principal industrial countries of the world and that its successful transfer depends upon "appropriate" compensation and suitable condition in the recipient country. Because of the latter factor, effective legal protection for industrial property rights needs to be assured and taxes are not to be imposed on license fees and royalties that have a near-confiscating nature. (10) Obviously, these views are not shared by the leadership of the Third World, which - in UNCTAD and other forums - has attacked the moral legitimacy of current industrial property rights.

The last section of the guidelines addresses itself to transfer pricing and commercial policies. It urges MNCs to practice fair pricing policies for goods and services in dealings with affiliated companies so as to take into consideration the tax, customs, and competition regulations of the countries involved. In general, no obstacles are to be placed by the MNC management to the development of the subsidiary's export business, and preference is to be given to competitive local sources of supply for components and raw materials for the production of goods, especially where the host country is an LDC. On the other hand, the investing MNC should not seek undue protection from competing imports or against competition from new manufacturers in worldwide and regional initiatives toward liberalization of international trade. It is doubtful whether the very broad fair-pricing provisions of the guidelines would satisfy Third World aspirations, or reciprocal trade liberalization measures would be acceptable after GATT has eliminated the principle of reciprocity for lowering tariffs when LDCs are involved. Nevertheless, the recognition of the potential evils of transfer pricing by the guidelines is more than a mere genuflection toward Third World demands and provides an initial basis for negotiations on this sensitive subject.

The ICC Court of Arbitration

Regardless of the quality of the ICC guidelines or any other code of conduct for MNCs, disputes among companies and between companies and governments concerning the interpretation of contractual arrangements or the practices and actions of nongovernmental and governmental actors are sure to arise. The ICC Court of Arbitration, founded more than 50 years ago, offers an international body to settle these disputes. The court has become a universally recognized authority, and now supervises arbitrations taking place all over the world. Over 100 new cases are submitted by business firms and governments each year, involving a large number of countries. These cases include disputes arising from contracts for public works, exclusive concessions, licenses of patents and know-how, and banking problems. At present, a large number of international public and private agreements provide for arbitration by the court in the event of disputes. Relying upon the proven strict neutrality of the court, many MNC executives consider acceptance of its arbitration facilities as proof of good faith, which justifies less rigid conditions in other clauses of the contract.

The court consists of a chairman, secretary-general, and technical advisors, plus members appointed by the ICC national committees, with each committee entitled to appoint one member. The neutrality of the court is strengthened by the rules requiring that the arbitrator (or the third arbitrator where there are three) must come from a country other than that of the parties, and the place of arbitration be fixed in a country other than that of the parties (unless otherwise agreed beforehand). The proceedings before the Court are secret. Legal enforcement of the award, if needed (which has been rare), can be assured by means of the New York Convention on the Recognition and Enforcement of Foreign Arbitral Awards, which has been ratified by more than 40 countries, including the United States, Soviet Union, many European states, and a number of developing countries. (11)

OECD GUIDELINES OF MNC CONDUCT

In the OECD Ministerial Declaration of June 21, 1976, adopting the Guidelines for MNC conduct, (12) no attempt was made - in contrast to the efforts of the United Nations Commission on Transnational Corporations - to elaborate any precise legal definition for multinational enterprises or corporations. Yet the guidelines offer some conception of MNCs according to which they

> usually comprise companies and other entities whose ownership is private, state or mixed, established in different countries and so linked that one or more of them may be able to exercise a significant influence over the activities of others and, in particular,

to share knowledge and resources with the others. The degree of autonomy of each entity in relation to the others varies widely from one multinational enterprise to another, depending on the nature of the links between such entities and the field of activity concerned. (13)

This concept is narrower and more useful than the initial definition used in the Report of the United Nations Group of Eminent Persons. (14)

Similar to the ICC, the OECD guidelines are addressed to both parent company and its affiliates in the host countries, and the word "enterprise" as used in the guidelines refers to the various entities in accordance with their particular responsibilities.

The guidelines stress the sovereignty principle in the relationship between states and MNC entities located within national boundaries. But while national governments can prescribe the conditions under which MNC units have to operate, they must respect international law and international agreements to which they are signatories. On the other hand, the guidelines themselves, though emanating jointly from the member governments of the OECD, are merely recommendations, whose "observation is voluntary and not legally enforced." Nevertheless, compliance is urged because it is likely "to strengthen the basis of mutual confidence between enterprises and States." (15)

As was already expressed by the ICC Guidelines, the OECD requests MNCs to take fully into account the general policy objectives of home and host countries, including aims and priorities for economic and social progress, the creation of employment opportunities, the promotion of indigenous technological progress, and the protection of the environment. There is a strong and broad injunction against rendering to and solicitation of bribes by any holder of public office, as well as against contributions to candidates for public office, political parties, or other political organizations unless the latter is "legally permissible." In general, MNCs should abstain from any "improper" involvement in local political actitities. (16)

The "full disclosure" provisions of the OECD code seek to lift the veil of secrecy used by MNCs to conceal their control over vast networks of companies that have different names, although they are part of an overall organization. As a consequence, MNCs are asked to make public complete descriptions of the activities of their principal affiliates in the various geographical areas of the world, including new capital investments, sources and uses of funds for operations and sales, operating results by area and particular products, the average number of employees in each area and total expenditures for research and development. Important for meeting the profound concern of Third World countries regarding MNC behavior is the request to bare their policies on intra-enterprise pricing.

Maximum competition is a main principle embodied in the OECD Guidelines. Major stress is placed upon the prevention of the abuse of dominant positions MNCs or their affiliates may hold in particular markets, countries, or regions. Examples given are:

(a) anticompetitive acquisitions,

(b) predatory behavior toward competitors,

(c) unreasonable refusal to deal,

(d) anticompetitive abuse of industrial property rights,

(e) discriminatory (i.e., unreasonably differentiated) pricing and using such pricing transactions between affiliated enterprises as a means of affecting adversely competition outside these enterprises. (17)

In addition, participation in international and domestic cartels as well as in restrictive agreements impeding competition is specifically mentioned as undesirable MNC behavior. Also, restrictions may not be imposed on the freedom of purchasers, distributors, and licensees to resell or export goods purchased from MNCs or their subsidiaries or produced under their licenses.

Under the heading of taxation, transfer pricing is again attacked unless it conforms to "arm's length" standards. Otherwise, it is likely to distort the tax base on which MNC units are assessed, to the disadvantage of the national authorities.

Relatively extensive space is devoted in the guidelines to employment and industrial relations. The main emphasis is on the insistence that MNCs should respect the right of their employees to organize into unions and to engage in collective bargaining. A special injunction is invoked against utilizing the ability of the MNC to transfer the whole or part of a production facility from one country to another as a threat to influence collective bargaining or the right of workers to organize. Other concerns are the upgrading of the labor force, a matter of major interest to Third World countries, and "reasonable notice" to employee representatives in case of closing-down operations that may involve layoffs. (18)

In the crucial area of technology transfer and science, the OECD guidelines are short, and whatever they say is phrased in general terms. MNCs are to ensure that their activities fit into the scientific and technological policies and plans of host countries and contribute to the development of national capabilities in science and technology, especially as far as innovative progress is concerned. Transfer of technology is to be carried out on "reasonable terms and conditions," but with due regard to the "protection of industiral and intellectual property rights." (19) Obviously, these recommendations fall far short of satisfying the demands and aspirations of Third World governments.

While the guidelines are addressed by the OECD member states exclusively to MNC managements, they contain policy directives for the governments of these countries as well. Moreover, the other two parts of the OECD package address themselves solely to the member governments. Nondiscriminatory national treatment of locally owned subsidiaries or affiliates controlled by foreign MNCs is the rule set, and any exception - including restrictions on new foreign investments that were in effect in June 1976 - had to be brought to the attention of the OECD within 60 days. New exceptions to nondiscriminatory treatment by member states and their territorial subdivisions must be reported within 30 days.

The third part of the package is designed to avoid interference of the flow of direct international investments. While it is recognized that national economic objectives and policies designed to redress regional economic imbalances may, from time to time, require the institution of specific incentives or disincentives with respect to foreign investment, the principle established is to hold such actions and their effects to a minimum.

The Committee on International Investment and Multinational Enterprise (CIME) is the body to periodically review the application of the guidelines as well as the implementation of the rules on national treatment and on incentives and disincentives. CIME will also serve as a forum of intergovermental consultation on these matters, if problems arise, and it will periodically invite business and labor groups to present their views on the functioning of the guidelines.

The 1979 Review

It is instructive to examine briefly the issues raised and problems encountered during the CIME review of the OECD guidelines. Similar issues and problems will likely surface during reviews that are planned for the prospective United Nations code of conduct.

One issue raised in the United States Department of State Advisory Committee on International Investment, Technology, and Development regarding the application of the guidelines was about the efforts of OECD governments to publicize the contents of the guidelines. Apparently, governments had made significant efforts to increase knowledge and and acceptance regarding the guidelines, including the United States, which cooperated with the business community in this respect. While all governments had recommended the guidelines to all MNCs, there is uncertainty regarding the form of acceptance. Overt acceptance has been spotty, although most firms may be complying with the guidelines, even without overt acceptance. Particular difficulties have arisen in getting state-owned enterprises to accept them. To overcome the confusion about acceptance and compliance, OECD may recommend that MNCs indicate their acceptance of the guidelines in their annual reports. However, it has not been decided whether this should be a one-time insertion in the annual report (the United States view), or an annual statement of how the MNC has applied the guidelines. (20) This method may also be useful for the United Nations code if it turns out to be a voluntary, nonbinding instrument.

Some attempts have been made since the inauguration of the guidelines to give a greater role to the Business and Industry Advisory Committee to OECD (BIAC) and the Trade Union Advisory Committee (TUAC) in problem solving on the international level. However, the governments opposed this proposal and emphasized that problems should be resolved on the national levels. Similarly, there has been little support for a formal OECD fact-finding mechanism. Finally, clarification of the guidelines, perhaps in the form of advisory opinions, should emanate mainly from the national level, although some issues may have to be referred to the OECD. (21) The rationale behind the opposition to greater involvement on the international level is the concern to maintain fully the voluntary nature of the guidelines. This could be impaired if, in the attempted resolution of problems with the application of the guidelines, specific conclusions were reached regarding the behavior of individual MNCs. Implementation and follow-up measures on the national level are preferred, perhaps because on this level the interests of firms can be safeguarded with maximum effectiveness. There may well be an inherent conflict between the philosophical basis for a voluntary code and the obvious need for follow-up mechanisms if the guidelines are to turn out to be nothing but a sham. The same, of course, also will apply to a voluntary United Nations code of conduct, and it is a difficult problem to resolve. (22)

Other, more substantive problem areas in the review process included consultation with governments when a firm disinvests, the relevance of profitability of a subsidiary in the event it is to be closed, and prior "consultation" with labor unions before a final decision is taken. Some members of the Working Group of the State Department Advisory Committee held on March 9, 1979, felt that the consultations with labor unions would be an infringement of what might be basically management decisions. European firms, more used to co-determination procedures with union representatives, may be more understanding of the consultation principle, even if they do not like it. Another member stated that profitability may not be the key factor relating to closing down a subsidiary. (23)

Despite the various issues raised, there was consensus that in order to preserve the credibility of the guidelines, no major changes in the text would be acceptable and that only minor modifications would be made to close undesired gaps in the document..

It is reasonable to assume that one of the OECD's purposes in drafting the guidelines was to head off Third World efforts to impose their very restrictive concepts upon MNCs through the elaboration of United Nations codes of conduct. This purpose has not been realized; nevertheless, the OECD guidelines have merit by themselves as the first major statement by the industrialized countries of the world about their expectations regarding the future behavior of MNCs everywhere. The guidelines may also motivate some developing countries to enact appropriate legislation that would bring about greater legal security for foreign investments and, at the same time, outlaw exploitative business practices in their countries. Indeed, if the enactment of such legislation were to spread, it would build common legal bases for the operation of international business gradually all over the world. But this may well remain an impossible dream, as we will see in the next, and last chapter.

9 Prospects and Implications for the Future

With the adoption of the OECD guidelines for MNCs and of the governmental policies on international investments, the Western industrialized countries have put forth their general positions on the behavior of multinational enterprises and have set up parameters for the treatment of MNC investments. As we have already noted, the OECD guidelines will not satisfy the demands of the Third World countries on regulating and supervising the conduct of MNCs. Therefore, no chance exists that they will be accorded general acceptance, although a few of the principles and some of the wording used in the guidelines has been adopted in the formulation for the United Nations code. Suggestions were made during the Intergovernmental Working Group sessions for the use of additional text from the guidelines for the purpose of clarification and consistency. The OECD guidelines did not address themselves to measures against corrupt practices, which have been strongly condemned, especially by the United States government. Since such measures must cover not only activities of MNC managements but also the behavior of government officials in all countries of the world, a broader forum than the OECD is needed and the proposed multilateral agreement on this subject has to be negotiated within the United Nations framework. Hence, in every respect the ball is now in the United Nations court.

THE PROSPECTS FOR UNITED NATIONS SUCCESS

What are the prospects for a resolution of the outstanding controversial issues regarding the general United Nations code as well as the other matters currently being negotiated in various United Nations bodies? We have seen in chapter 6 that the gap between the Third World countries and the Western group has narrowed considerably on the

117

substance for a transfer of technology code, while work on the general code of conduct has also made progress, even though major parties remain apart on several crucial issues. We should also note that progress on the technology-transfer issue is closely related to changes in foreign-policy positions of major powers, especially of the United States toward the Third World, Africa in particular. On the other hand, some Third World leaders seem to have shown more down-to-earth attitudes, contributing to enhanced prospects for overcoming the divergencies in the field. It may well have been with this progress in mind that the group of Western industrialized countries issued a statement at the conclusion of the Nairobi UNCTAD conference which declared inter alia:

> We believe that a code can be produced which will make a major positive contribution to the international transfer of technology, as well as to strengthening the technological capacity of all States, especially developing countries. (1)

Agreement on the substance of the technology-transfer issue will be affected by the efforts of Third World countries to revise the existing conventions on patents and trademarks, in particular the Paris Convention of 1883. (2) In the forefront of these efforts is the World Intellectual Property Organization (WIPO), which closely cooperates with UNCTAD. Although a resolution passed by the Nairobi Conference (UNCTAD IV) gave strong backing for these revisions, and especially the recommendations made by WIPO experts, it is doubtful that the Western industrialized countries would consent to any changes of the Paris Convention which would weaken the basic principle of the protection of industrial and intellectual property rights. However, the possession of rights may also impose certain obligations, and these obligations could well include positive responses to obvious technological needs of the poor countries and the abstention from the abuse of patent rights.

As for possible agreement on the substance of a general code of conduct, a comparison between the initial positions of the group of Western countries and those of the Group of "77" with the working group chairman's formulations presented in chapter 5 reveals that many of the earlier disparities have been narrowed, if not fully bridged. (3)

Especially in the field of labor and employment, considerable consensus exists, but special provisions are also found in other areas. In the areas relating to jurisdiction and sovereignty, including the concept of "permanent" sovereignty over natural resources, the Group of "77" delegates have taken a very hard stand. Moreover, they have displayed a very high level of solidarity on all issues, despite the fact that their interests may diverge. Such states as Mexico, Brazil, and Singapore have reached a much more advanced level of economic development and sophistication than many of the very poor countries in Africa and Central America. Nevertheless, opportunities for compromise may exist in the more difficult areas, but reaching agreements will depend on several factors independent of the merit of individual compromise proposals. These factors are: (a) success in solving most technology transfer issues within UNCTAD, (b) changes in policy views on the part of the participating governments toward MNC activities, and by the Western countries toward the Third World, (c) sincere give-and-take attitudes, especially by Third World countries, and (d) tolerant understanding of the domestic-political environment within which all governments must operate.

THE APPLICABILITY AND LEGAL NATURE OF THE CODES

Perhaps a much more troublesome problem than trying to overcome the divergencies on the substance of the codes is determination as to whether they are to apply exclusively to MNCs or also to nation-states and whether compliance is to be voluntary or mandatory. The OECD guidelines, as we have seen, were directed only to MNCs, but the Group of Eminent Persons recommended that the prospective code of conduct address itself to governments as well. (4) This is also the position taken by the United States, which insists that the responsibilities of governments and MNCs in the code must be balanced and must apply to state-owned enterprises regardless of whether they operate as profit-making entities or not. Although it may be contended that placing the MNCs and governments on the same level as far as compliance is concerned would violate the principle of sovereignty, held so dear by many Third World countries, a good argument can be made for the recommendation of the group. From our discussion in the preceding chapters, it is evident that tensions between MNCs' host and home countries arise because of the impredictability and unfairness of governmental actions and behavior. This happens in the preinvestment decision-making phase as well as after subsidiaries have been established and have been in operation for some time. The governmental action producing malaise and problems may range from uncertainty about incentive tax advantages prior to investment to the suspension of profit repatriation later on. There is no valid reason why governments should not subject themselves to appropriate rules on these matters. Taxation and repatriation are proper subjects for inclusion in bilateral agreements and such inclusion would prevent or reduce unnecessary MNC-government tensions. (5) The OECD directives to member governments on indiscriminatory treatment of foreign investments and on the investment incentives and disincentives are a good beginning. The prospective code must also not become a basis for discriminatory action against MNCs. MNCs and domestic firms have to be given equitable treatment in accordance with international law.

The legal nature of the code or codes is most likely to be the most contested matter. For the Group of "77" countries, supported by the communist countries, only a mandatory code can be effective in assuring that MNCs will contribute to the attainment of national policy goals and the objectives enshrined in the New International Economic

Order. For MNC managements - backed by the Western industrialized countries -a compulsory code is anathema. (6) Of course, even in the unlikely event that agreement could be reached on a mandatory code, the question of enforcement would prove to be difficult, as we have already seen in chapter 7.

If the code were adopted in the form of a multilateral treaty, it would entail ratification by each United Nations member state according to that state's constitution and could be a very long process. Noncompliance by a national government, if the code would be made applicable to them, could make them subject to retaliatory economic measures according to the particular provisions of the treaty as well as to adverse publicity. The provisions of the code addressed to MNCs and their subsidiaries would most likely be incorporated into the national legal systems of the countries adhering to the multilateral treaty. The provisions, therefore, could be enforced in the national courts. If, in the event of violation of the code's provisions, court action is not initiated by the state's authorities, its government would expose itself to the countervailing measures mentioned above. For situations in which the codes are embodied in international instruments other than a treaty (for example, a declaration passed by the United Nations General Assembly) enforcement would be through appeals to fairness and justice and sanctions such as unfavorable public opinion (black lists), or some other type of adverse measures by other countries or even MNCs. These sanctions would apply to violation of the code by MNC or their affiliates as well as by governments if they had been made addressee of the code's provisions. Consultation mechanisms among governments, conducted within the United Nations framework, may also be useful to ensure adherence to the code. A number of consultative mechanisms will be acceptable to the United States, (7) although specifics have not been determined.

Since in all probability the technology-transfer code will be completed first, its legal status may well decide the status of the general code of conduct as well. But when can completion of these codes be expected? Considering the remaining divergencies in views and consequent impasses, the technology transfer code is not likely to be finished before 1980 or 1981, and estimates for the time to complete the general code range to as much as five years. With the legal nature of the codes being a major obstacle to agreement, completion may depend on how urgently the Third World wants to see codes of conduct materialize. Since the resistance to a mandatory instrument on the part of the Western governments and the MNCs is extremely high and probably insurmountable, a voluntary code may be acceptable by the LDCs, at least initially, if some monitoring and consultation activities could be institutionalized. For the LDCs this may signify a step in the direction of achieving the NIEO and the Charter of Economic Rights and Duties of States, which contain major goals of the Group of "77." Without doubt, it has become clear to the leadership of this group that these goals can only be attained on a step-by-step basis in different international forums and through a variety of incremental activities.

There is also the possibility that on certain substantive subjects of the codes, agreement will be impossible because opposing positions are held so strongly that reconciliation cannot be achieved. Under such circumstances, provisions relating to these subjects might be left out entirely and the instrument drafted may be a partial code of a voluntary nature.

If the initial instrument would be either a complete or partial code, an evolutionary process may be set in motion. Assuming that the provisions of the codes are reasonable and fair, they are likely to find acceptance by MNCs and governments and may well be generally adhered to. The codes will acquire legitimacy on their own and may gradually evolve through custom into binding rules. Under such conditions, enforcement of compliance would hardly be necessary and would not present many problems if violation were to occur. Also, because of this process, agreement on the missing provisions of a partial code might be reached more easily and the code could be eventually completed.

Whether such a scenario is realistic will depend on the interest in the code on the part of the major groupings. The developed countries of the West have never been overly enthusiastic about the code, despite the fact that a majority of these are more often host countries than states where MNCs are headquartered. Some of the Western countries and probably all MNCs would be just as happy if the drawn-out negotiations and discussions would come to nought, despite official assertion of deep commitment to the completion of the code. However, the Group of "77" seems very intent to arrive at a concrete result, although the outcome may fall short of their initial expectations. As long as the push toward the NIEO remains viable, the project of the code or codes is likely to have a high priority.

For most of the Western countries, the code also has foreign-policy implications with respect to the Third World that cannot be ignored. They have a definite foreign policy interest to respond as favorably as possible to the Third World demands for NIEO implementation, and the drafting of these codes must be seen in this light. Representatives of MNCs, business groups, and labor unions who are members of the various advisory groups to foreign policy officials in the United States and other Western countries must keep this in mind. In this connection, it is important to stress that many MNCs have fully recognized that criticism of some of their activities in host and home countries were justified. Indeed, more than 200 MNCs, mostly in the United States, have developed their own codes of conduct, which exhort their executives to perform their management functions and general business affairs in an ethical manner, to abide by all laws of home and host countries and to demonstrate exemplary citizenship. Some of these codes are quite lengthy, covering many phases of MNC operations, with which the United Nations code of conduct is expected to deal. The Caterpillar Tractor Company code is an example. Others address themselves mainly to problems of corrupt practices. Enforcement of these codes is, of course, up to the individual MNC, which must supervise its own personnel and activities. (8)

POSSIBILITIES OF PARALLEL NATIONAL
LEGISLATION AND INVESTMENT REGULATIONS

In our discussion of the OECD guidelines we mentioned the optimistic attitude that the principles embodied in these guidelines might inspire efforts at the enactment of parallel or concurrent national legislation on foreign investments and other MNC activities. If such efforts would be undertaken on an extensive scale, a network of uniform regulations could emerge, guiding the behavior of governments of both host and home countries as well as of MNCs. Greater predictability of governmental actions would make MNC investment and other management decisions easier by injecting a higher level of rationality. It could avoid misunderstandings between MNC units and national governments and easily dispel them after they had arisen.

Up to now, efforts to enact parallel legislation affecting the relations between governments and MNCs are relatively rare. Apart from the OECD directives on international investments mentioned earlier, the foreign investment laws of the six member states of the Andean Common Market constitute the most comprehensive endeavor to regulate investment policy and incentives, taxation, exchange of information, and the regional protection of industrial policy. Other regional organizations, such as the African and Malagasy Common Organization (OCAM) and the Caribbean Community, have attempted to enact common rules on a few selected MNC activities, but the effectiveness of these regulations is open to doubt, and some lack ratification by the member states. The OAS has been pondering the problem as well as the possible development of a code of conduct of its own.

Nevertheless, while parallel or concurrent national legislation relating to MNC activities is sparse, a good number of countries have some regulations on different aspects of these activities. The Secretariat of the United Nations Commission on Transnational Corporations has issued a detailed report and analysis which is very useful for MNC executives and academicians. (9)

With respect to the Third World, the report states that national foreign-investment legislation is far from uniform and displays great variation in approaches, objectives, and comprehensiveness, as well as in the extent of the regulation, control, and discrimination to which it subjects direct foreign investment. This should not be surprising in view of the great disparities in size and capabilities of the developing countries. The practice of case-by-case negotiations of investment agreements is widely used. In this connection, we should note that the Department of Economic and Social Affairs of the United Nations, at the request of governments of some of the developing countries, has provided some advisory service to over 20 countries since 1971. This advisory service has covered matters relating to direct private foreign investment and other forms of foreign business participation. (10) However, there appears now to be a tendency toward the consolidation of legislation on direct foreign investments, and in due time this may reduce the need for special United Nations personnel to assist in individual negotiations.   Investment incentives play a major role in all Third World investment policies, and in a few cases the regulation of investment schemes is the only significant body of rules of national legislation on MNC activities.

Although there is a definite trend in the Third World to insist on local participation in the ownership of foreign enterprises, the proportion of countries that insist on majority local ownership is as yet relatively small. While most developing countries have at least made a policy commitment to the indigenization of management, action in this direction appears to have been limited, partly because suitably qualified personnel are scarce. (11)

Other subject matters of national-investment legislation include the prohibition or restriction of foreign investments in certain critical sectors, the repatriation of profits, access to local credit facilities, taxation, control of local MNC operations, nationalization, and the settlement of disputes. The administration of the legislation, an important facet of its effectiveness, is handled mostly by interministerial investment boards or commissions and sometimes by special agencies established for the purpose of coordinating all matters relating to foreign investment. Because adequate means for implementation and supervision of the regulations are often not available in Third World countries, administrative effectiveness is sometimes very low. (12)

The comission report distinguishes three general patterns of direct foreign-investment legislation. One general pattern, which prevails in most African and certain Asian countries as well as in the Central American Common Market, is characterized by relatively few regulations and restrictions and a greater number of incentives. Most countries in this group accept international dispute-settlement procedures such as those provided by the International Center for Settlement of Investment Disputes of the World Bank.

The second pattern is found in the Asian Middle East and North Africa and is primarily a variation of the first pattern, except that most countries have established local participation quotas. There is greater discrimination against foreign enterprises in the regulation of investment, and incentives are for shorter time periods and mainly awarded only for new installations.

The third pattern predominating in South America includes the following features: (a) case-by-case screening for all foreign investments with relatively few tax incentives, (b) limitations on foreign managerial control and special screenings for technology transfers, (c) repatriation ceilings on profits, royalties, and other fees and regulations for debt financing, and (d) local adjudication of investment disputes. (13)

More details about these patterns can be found in table 9.1, which is self-explanatory. While the successful completion and adoption of a general code of conduct would result in uniform - and in many instances stricter - general rules, individual countries or regional organizations may retain their own regulations.

TABLE 9.1. Patterns of Direct Foreign Investment Regulations in Selected Developing Countries

Parameter	Pattern I (mostly Asia - excluding India-Africa, CACMO)	Pattern II (mostly Middle East North Africa)	Pattern III (mostly South America)
I. Administration	Case-by-case screening largely restricted to award of incentives (nondiscriminatory).	Case-by-case screening at establishment (degree of discrimination varies).	Separate administration for foreign investment. Screening at establishment.
II. Investment screening criteria	Emphasis on functional contributions of investment. Little indication of extensive cost-benefit analysis. Screening largely for award of incentives.	Emphasis on functional contributions and conditions of investment. Little indication of extensive cost-benefit analysis.	Criteria formulated for cost-benefit analysis, often extensive. Includes social cost criteria in some cases.
III. Ownership	Few requirements. Few sectors closed to foreign investment.	Joint ventures prevalent.	Strict regulations on ownership and investment (exc. Brazil). A large number of closed sectors.
IV. Finance	Few repatriation limitations.	Few repatriation limitations.	Repatriation ceilings in most areas (exc. Mexico). Screening of foreign loans. Special control of payments to parent company.
V. Employment and training	Announced indigenization policies but little headway in practice.	Local quotas for work force. Few local quotas for management.	Specific across-the-board indigenization requirements.
VI. Technology transfer	No controls.	No controls.	Screening and registration of all technology imported.
VII. Investment	Long-term tax incentives for establishment.	Establishment incentives limited to five years - in most cases nonrenewable.	Incentives tied to specific contributions, but incentives may be curtailed for foreign owned firms.
VIII. International dispute settlement	Adherence to international regulation. Regional investment regulation: UDEAC, OCAM, EAC.*	Same as Pattern I. Regional investment regulation: Arab Economic Union.	Local adjudication and regional harmonization of investment regulation: ANCOM, CACM.

*For practical purposes the East African Community has ceased to exist.

Source: UN ECOSOC Document E/C.10/8, January 12, 1976, pp. 21, 22.

THE IMPLICATIONS

If we review the moves made in the United Nations since the beginning of the 1970s regarding MNC-Third World interactions and evaluate the discussions and negotiations in the Group of Eminent Persons, the Commission on Transnational Corporations, and in UNCTAD, we cannot help but characterize the relationship between Third World countries on one side and Western countries and MNCs on the other as "adversary," despite the less confrontational atmosphere in the commission, inter-governmental working groups, and UNCTAD during the last few years. The communist countries generally supported the views and aspirations of the Third World. As we have seen, some progress has been made in both of these bodies toward reconciliation of opposing viewpoints, and American foreign policy has assumed a much more accommodating stance toward Third World demands for general development assistance within the framework of the New Economic International Order and specifically toward LDC positions on technology transfer and MNC activities. But as strong anti-MNC attitudes appear to linger on among many Third World representatives, suspicion and distrust continue to contaminate the United Nations atmosphere. Under such conditions, the elaboration of fair and reasonable codes of conduct are made considerably more difficult than under a prevailing climate of confidence and trust.

GROWING INTEREST DIVERGENCE AMONG LDCs

We have noted earlier that the economic interests of LDCs do not coincide and that this divergence is growing. A number of Third World countries have staged an extraordinary upward movement in their economies during 1977 through proper import substitution by investing about 25 percent of their national income in various manufacturing plants and materially expanding the export of manufactured goods. Generally included in this group are Brazil, Mexico, South Korea, Taiwan, Hong Kong, and Singapore. These countries are called the New Industrial Countries (NIC), and their GNP has increased to 8.2 percent in 1977, about double the rate of the OECD countries. Concentrating their efforts in sectors where their low labor costs enable them to outsell their competitors, the NIC group now accounts for more than half of the industrial production of all Third World countries and three quarters of their manufactured exports. The investment climate for MNCs is generally favorable, although varying government regulations impose restrictions on the establishment and operation of MNC affiliates. (14)

As the economic trend of the NICs continues and as some of them become home countries of MNCs (as is beginning to happen in Brazil and elsewhere), their governments may consider shifts of policy that would approach the policies pursued by the Western industrialized countries. However, such a policy shift will be slow, as their quest for full autonomy of choice remains overshadowing. The elites in the NICs may vigorously oppose any perceived threat to this autonomy. (15) This most likely is the reason for the persistent Group of "77" solidarity, which we have observed in the negotiations on the different United Nations codes of conduct. Indeed, political enemies have buried their differences in MNC issues and taken a common stand; for example, Iraq with Syria, Ethiopia with Somalia, India with Pakistan, Zaire with Angola, and Brazil with Cuba. (16)

In order to bypass the problem of the slow code completion, yet benefit from new MNC investments while establishing a set of rules for such investments, LDCs may negotiate bilateral investment treaties with MNC home countries. This has been done successfully by a number of European countries with more than 50 LDCs. The United States is also interested in such treaties, which would contain provisions on national treatment of MNCs, standards for expropriation and compensation, rules for financial flows, and mechanisms for dispute settlement and consultations. The treaties would foster an enhanced climate for investment by providing United States MNCs with recognized ground rules and by promoting a stable system of international law and commitment in the field of investment protection.

The question arises whether the desire of an LDC to negotiate a bilateral treaty signals a decline or complete lack of interest in the United Nations' endeavors for codes of conduct. Undoubtedly, the negotiation of such a treaty normally takes place in a more serene environment than can be expected under the pressure-laden circumstances in which the United Nations code of conduct discussions and bargaining unfold. However, the strong feeling of solidarity that pervades all Third World countries makes it unlikely that the interest of any LDC in the codes will slacken, even if it should sign a bilateral treaty on investment. On the other hand, if bilateralism should grow extensively, it could become a substitute for a code for industrial countries, since such a system of bilateral treaties would provide a measure of predictability for governments and MNCs. For example, article 24 of the Andean Common Market Pact imposes strict requirements of a divestiture program on new MNC investments so as to shift majority ownership and control into local hands. Foreign participation in public utilities, the communication industries, banking, and the raw materials sector is very limited. Restrictions exist on licensing agreements and loans between foreign MNCs and local subsidiaries to prevent draining off of excessive profits. However, these provisions are not being applied uniformly by the members of the Andean Common Market. Chile, before withdrawing from Ancom, disregarded the provisions during most of the period of its membership. Colombia and other members have taken advantage of every loophole to weaken the spirit of article 24. Even Peru, which initially was the strongest proponent of the provisions, now shies away from strict application. (17)

In Southeast Asia, investment laws are often not strictly applied or completely ignored. In Thailand and Indonesia, joint ventures require local majority ownership, but the shareholders are frequently "dummies" or "nominal" shareholders who receive money for their shares from the foreign MNC and vote or behave in management functions as told by the MNC representatives. (18)   In Malaysia, there are requirements that indigenous managers must be hired by MNC subsidiaries.   But Malaysians with the required skills are hard to find, and if they are found, they often move from company to company, falling into a role that is more symbolic than substantive.   Similar problems of investment-law application also exist in Indonesia. (19)

THIRD WORLD MISCALCULATIONS?

In the zealous pursuit of their objective to devise MNC codes of conduct that would serve the implementation of the New International Economic Order, Third World governmental leaders, their representatives in United Nations bodies, and some United Nations officials may have made some serious miscalculations. There is considerable doubt that as J. Irwin Miller, Board Chairman of Cummins Engine Company and a member of the Group of Eminent Persons, stated: "Developing countries can count on the indiscriminate eagerness of all multinational corporations to invest in any developing nation." (20)   Indeed, many LDCs may assume incorrectly that they are attractive targets for MNC investments. There are several reasons for this misconception:

1. The accumulation of private capital in the Western industrialized countries has slowed down, and this trend is likely to continue in the foreseeable future. Investment funds may well be rationed and high-risk investments are likely to have low priorities even for natural resource developments when they are envisioned for LDCs with hostile investment climates.   For example, Exxon's halted exploration in Malaysia in 1975 and cut out plans for installation of oil production platforms in offshore Malaysian waters. (21)   Clearly, the philosophy of "growth at any cost," formerly espoused by many MNC managements, has given way again to a careful calculation of costs, risks, and profits. The growing number of expropriations, which amounted to 468 from 1969 to 1969 and rose to 979 from 1970 to 1976, makes investments in certain LDCs quite unattractive, although in relation to the total number of MNC affiliates the percentage of expropriations is fairly low. (22)

2. The incentive of low wages for American and some European MNCs to set up production facilities in foreign countries is slowly disappearing in the developed world. Since the early 1970s, average hourly wages in Sweden, Belgium, Germany, and Japan have begun to exceed those in the United States. While in developing countries such as Mexico and Taiwan a considerable wage differential vis-a-vis North

America and Western Europe continues to exist, the pay for workers has risen there also and is likely to rise further, particularly if unionization makes progress. In the meantime, the flow of investment funds from United States MNCs to Europe has diminished, while European and Japanese investments in new production facilities in the United States has risen substantially since 1974. In fact, some American MNCs have abandoned or sold a variety of manufacturing operations. (23)   This development has eased the apprehension of American organized labor about the alleged exportation of jobs, although MNCs have often denied this and contended that, on the contrary, going overseas has preserved or even increased jobs in the United States.   They point out that production facilities abroad have been drawing imports from the United States in the form of parts or raw materials.   However, the issue remains controversial, and consideration of space does not permit further explanation here.

3. An important motivation for investments by MNCs in foreign plants has been a variety of trade restrictions making it impossible for goods imported from third countries to compete successfully in national markets.   However, tariff and nontariff barriers have been gradually lowered, the successful Kennedy and Tokyo Rounds being outstanding examples of this trend.   On some products, tariffs have been eliminated completely.

4. Some of the home country governments, prodded by domestic political forces, may begin to tax profits generated in host countries even if they are already taxed abroad on the same level as in home countries.   The United States Congress has begun chipping away at the alleged tax advantage of American MNCs and may go further, with the result that the cost of foreign investment will increase.   Such double taxation could well reduce the appeal of international production and marketing activities. (24)   Proper tax harmonization among parent and host countries may be necessary to restore interest in setting up additional MNC subsidiaries in new countries.

The above factors will tend to reduce the willingness of MNC managements to accept United Nations endeavors to guide and perhaps regulate their investment and operational decisions.   Rules of MNC conduct perceived as interfering too much with normal business practices as well as intensive efforts to solicit business information exceeding usual disclosure customs are likely to be resisted and would be an exercise in futility.   Only a balanced set of fair rules that take into consideration the legitimate interests, traditional practices, and natural spheres of responsibility of MNCs and governments will produce beneficial results and make United Nations involvement a productive enterprise.   It seems impossible that the LDCs can impose any other kind of code of conduct on MNCs and the Western industrialized countries, and any rhetoric disregarding these principles will only be counterproductive to the redress of justified grievances suffered by Third World countries and populations.   It will make investment in older established industrial societies more attractive than investment in the developing societies of greater need, and MNCs are likely to make new investments only in those LDCs where the political climate is relatively friendly and where a high degree of predictability prevails as to the future of their investments. On the other hand, they may not object to a gradual transfer of ownership over a number of years if the terms are spelled out clearly, if profitable operations and experienced management continuity are assured, and if adequate payments for the transfer of shares to indigenous owners can be anticipated with confidence.

If generally acceptable codes of conduct could be evolved embodied in some kind of international instrument, American foreign policy toward the Third World may well benefit. Such codes would provide LDC governments with a clear map for future relationships with MNCs that in itself would instill in the Third World leadership a higher degree of self-confidence and gradually reduce the tendency of identifying all MNC misdeeds with American policy objectives. If the United States government were to narrow or completely eliminate the extraterritorial reach of its laws as a result of the codes (hardly a likely prospect), the American image may be further improved. On the other hand, very few LDCs have done anything to ensure the competitiveness of their own economies and are not ready to place antitrust regulations on their own firms, especially if a large number is partly or wholly owned by the state.

Through the codes, new attractive investment opportunities will be opened for American MNCs, and this use of private capital may lower the need for public funds for foreign-aid grants or loans. Forceful support of acceptable codes by the United States will be evidence that the comprehensive new policies toward the Third World announced by former Secretary of State Kissinger in his speeches during the Seventh Special Session of the United Nations General Assembly and UNCTAD IV in Nairobi, which have also been pursued by the Carter Administration, (25) are more than pleasant rhetoric and represent meaningful initiatives. If, however, no agreement on the codes of conduct for MNCs and governments can be reached, frustrations and discriminations will intensify, making implementation of the new American policies all the more difficult.

THE PROBLEM OF INTERDEPENDENCE ASYMETRY

Let us now return to the issue of interdependence and the constraints placed upon, as well as consequences for, entities caught up in the interdependence web. Our analysis of the protracted struggle revolving around the drafting of the codes of conduct in the United Nations reveals that it is closely linked to perceptions of dependence held by Third World governmental leaders vis-a-vis the arsenal of powers available to MNCs. These perceptions are intensified because of the realization that MNCs do possess the capabilities to offer solutions to serious LDC economic and even social problems. On the other hand, the

legal and political authority with which LDC governments are endowed
represents a capability to place constraints on MNC managements over
the establishment of affiliate facilities in a particular country. These
constraints might entail economic and managerial costs too high for the
pursuit of the MNCs' primary objective of profit maximization. The
potential incompatibility fo LDC and MNC objectives and the disparity
in perceptions regarding benefits and costs flowing from MNC practices
and governmental actions is complicated by the fact that a number of
LDCs possess large amounts of natural resources critical to the smooth
functioning of the industrial apparatus in the Western industrialized
countries. This substantially intensifies the already existing vast
asymmetry in the North-South interdependence relationship and heightens
the tensions between governments and MNCs built up over the years.

Another factor compounding the relationship between LDCs and
MNCs is the ability of governments to seize or issue particular
directives to a sensitive part of an MNC network and thereby obtain the
potential of influencing the rest of the network as well. For example,
Mexico insists that its foreign-owned automobile plants export their
components to other markets, which reduces exports of these parts
normally carried out by the Detroit or Sao Paolo facilities of the same
MNC. If the United States or Brazilian governments were to make
similar demands on the MNC's management for the exports of
components, the latter would be faced with very difficult problems. (26)

Successful engineering of codes of conduct is likely to help in the
objective reduction of the interdependence asymmetry by gradual
synchronization of MNC and governmental capabilities. But perhaps
more important, it may well moderate or completely suppress LDC
perceptions of dependency and inferiority and produce images of
greater compatibility of MNC goals and national policy objectives of
Third World countries. But this scenario may be too optimistic despite
compromises reached, and the possibility of additional compromises and
ultimately the United Nations efforts for elaborating codes may fail.
This would not be too surprising in view of the mistrust that, while
perhaps declining, seems to continue to pervade much of the negotiations. A basic suspicion prevails that whatever the Western industrialized countries may propose, the underlying motive may be
exploitation, and that LDCs will continue to be looked down upon in a
manner not much different from colonial times. Third World leaders
want to overcome these preindependence attitudes of many in the
Western world and are anxious to be treated with dignity so they can
gain and retain their self-respect. Thus, they strive for maximum
autonomy and want to nail down highly visible manifestations of
independence when the codes of conduct are drawn up. Interdependence
is seen by some as a strategy for continued enslavement as well as
cheap euphemism for dependence. Economic issues may well be less
important than the psychological issues, and independence more desired
than economic progress. (27) Such attitudes are not helpful for
achieving agreements on the codes.

Home country governments are also under pressure not only from

MNC headquarters, but also from other domestic political groups - including business associations and organized labor - to curtail "give-aways" of technology and other concessions perceived as contrary to the national interest. The State Department regularly consults on code-of-conduct questions with advisory committees composed of representatives of groups having a specific interest in the subject matter. Some of the other Western industrialized countries may have similar arrangements. The result is extensive circumspection before agreement on specific code issues and particular phrases is reached, and slow overall progress with many frustrations by all negotiating parties.

Regardless of whether ultimately codes of conduct for MNCs and governments can be elaborated, Perlmutter and Sagahafi-nejad have pointed to a positive aspect of the protracted negotiations, even if they should ultimately fail. (28) This positive and hopeful aspect is the initiation of a learning process for all participants in the negotiations, giving them opportunities to learn what the real issues and interests are and who are the key actors. They are acquiring detailed knowledge about the implications of the various proposed formulations. As a consequence, tendencies toward engaging in idle rhetoric are reduced. Despite differences in political and economic power, the bargaining between delegates seems to have acquired an egalitarian flavor, and the need for pragmatic results is recognized by the negotiators. I share the view that the negotiations have been and continue to be a valuable learning process, and this view is now accepted by many observers.

One of the most fundamental barriers to the successful drafting codes of conduct in the various United Nations bodies remains the very strong accent on the principle of sovereignty, although this emphasis is very understandable in the case of the newly independent countries of the Third World. Nevertheless, as Pierre Uri states so aptly:

> ...nothing ample enough will be achieved as long as in the United Nations the emphasis remains on "nations" rather than on "united"; as long as the debates continue in terms of a transfer of power which is unacceptable to some and inaccessible to others; as long as countries will not in their daily dealings prove really aware of their interdependence, even in their relations with the weakest of them. Intentions are reaffirmed each time like litanies in which the layman is hard put to perceive progress towards agreement which has required so much diplomatic subtlety. One cheerfully underwrites hundreds of principles without ever taking actual steps to translate them into realities. (29)

Let us hope that the code negotiators can avoid this tendency toward nonaction and that United Nations politics associated with the achievement of the NIEO and the Charter of Economic Rights and Duties of States does not become a trap for the code endeavors.

Notes

CHAPTER 1

(1) For an excellent review of the literature, see Elizabeth Crump Hanson, "Theoretical Perspectives on the Multinational Corporation: A Synthesis" (Paper presented at the 1976 Annual Meeting of the International Studies Association, Toronto, Canada, February 27, 1976).

(2) For more restrictive concepts, see Werner J. Feld, Nongovernmental Forces and World Politics (New York: Praeger, 1972), pp. 22-23 and the footnotes listed there. Additional definitional issues will be discussed in later chapters.

(3) Fortune (May and August 1978).

(4) Howard V. Perlmutter, "Towards Research on and Development of Nations" (Address before the symposium on "International Collective Bargaining" sponsored by the International Institute of Labour Studies of the ILO, April 29, 1969, Geneva, Switzerland).

(5) Feld, Nongovernmental Forces, pp. 84-91.

(6) Ibid.

(7) It has become fashionable to identify also a Fourth and perhaps Fifth World depending on the economic status of a particular less-developed country. The poorest of them belongs to the last category.

(8) United States Department of State, Toward a Strategy of Interdependence, Bureau of Public Affairs, no. 17, July 1975.

(9) See Kenneth F. Waltz, "The Myth of National Interdependence," in The Intranational Corporation, ed. Charles P. Kindleberger (Cambridge, Mass.: The M.I.T. Press, 1970), pp. 205-23, on p. 206.

(10) For differing views see, for example, Louis Turner, The Invisible Empires (New York: Harcourt, Brace, 1971); Howard V. Perlmutter, "The Multinational Firm and the Future," The Annals of the American Academy 403 (September 1972): 139-52; and Samuel Pisar in Realities, February 1972, pp. 38-44. See also Harry Magdoff, The Age of Imperialism: The Economics of U.S. Foreign Policy (New York: Monthly Review Press, 1969); Elizabeth R. Jager, "The Conglomerate Goes Global," AFL-CIO American Federationist, January 1970; Peter F. Drucker, "Multinationals and Developing Countries: Myths and Realities," C. Fred Bergesten, "Coming Investment Wars?" and Joseph S. Nye, Jr., "Multinational Corporations in World Politics," all in Foreign Affairs 53 (October 1974): 122-34, 135-52, and 153-75 respectively.

(11) See Waltz, "The Myth of National Interdependence," and Richard Rosecrance and Arthur Stein, "Independence: Myth or Reality," in World Politics 26 (October 1973): 1-27.

(12) Oran Young, "Interdependencies in World Politics," International Journal, Autumn 1969, p. 726.

(13) Edward L. Morse, "Transnational Economic Processes," International Organization 25 (Summer 1971): 373-97, on 379.

(14) Richard N. Cooper, The Economics of Interdependence (New York: McGraw Hill, 1968), pp. 3-8.

(15) Waltz, "The Myth of National Interdependence," pp. 205-207. See also the interesting empirical study by R. Rosecrance, A. Alexandroff, W. Koehler, S. Lagueur, and J. Stocker, "Wither Interdependence?" International Organization 31 (Summer 1977): 425-71. The authors come to the conclusion that "the pattern of contemporary interdependence is much more mixed than many have believed" and that data from recent years indicate a gradual and progressive detachment of individual national policies for the general trend toward interdependence (pp. 441-42).

(16) William D. Coplin and Michael K. O'Leary, "A Policy Analysis Framework for Research, Education, and Policy-Making in International Relations" (Paper presented at the 1974 Annual Meeting of the International Studies Association, St. Louis, Missouri), p. 22.

(17) Robert O. Keohane and Joseph S. Nye, "World Politics and the International Economic System in The Future of the International Economic Order, ed. C. Fred Bergstein (Lexington, Mass.: D.C. Heath, 1973), pp. 115-80.

(18) Keohane and Nye, "World Politics and the International Economic System," p. 124.

(19) See United Nations Department of Economic and Social Affairs, Multinational Corporations in World Development (New York: Praeger, 1974), pp. 5-6.

(20) In Brazil, outflows have shifted in inflows, reflecting a slowdown in economic activity there and the effect of regulations designed to discourage affiliate imports. See Ralph Kozlow, John Rutter, and Patricia Walker, "U.S. Direct Investment Abroad," U.S. Department of Commerce, Survey of Current Business 58 (August 1978): 16-38, on p. 19.

(21) See David H. Galler, "Capital Expenditures by Majority-Owned Foreign Affiliates," U.S. Department of Commerce, Survey of Current Business 58 (March 1978): 25-30.

(22) See J.P. Curhan, W.H. Davidson, and R. Suri, Tracing the Multinationals (Cambridge, Mass.: Ballinger, 1977), pp. 19-23.

(23) For details on recipient countries, see United Nations Economic and Social Council, Transnational Corporations in World Development: A Re-examination (E/C.10/38), 1978, table III-49.

(24) Ibid., table III-43.

(25) A vast literature on the issue of Third World dependency has evolved during the last few years. For example, the entire issue of International Organization, vol. 32, Winter 1978, is devoted to dependency and dependence with five articles focusing on theoretical aspects and four dealing with regional problems. See also Richard B. Fagan, "Studying Latin American Politics: Some Implications of a Dependence Appraoch," Latin American Research Review 12 (1977): 3-26; Robert R. Kaufman, Harry I. Chermotsky, and Daniel S. Geller, "A Preliminary Test of the Theory of Dependence," Comparative Politics 7 (April 1975): 303-30; Benjamin Cohen, The Question of Imperialism (New York: Basic Books, 1973), which is a critical analysis of dependency theory; and Thomas Moran, Multinational Corporations and the Politics of Dependence (Princeton, N.J.: Princeton University Press, 1974).

(26) See Hayward R. Alker, Jr., Lincoln P. Bloomfield, Nazli Choucri, Analyzing Global Interdependence, vol. 2 (Cambridge, Mass.: Center for International Studies, M.I.T., 1974), p. 2.

(27) Toward a Strategy of Interdependence.

(28) United States Department of State, Bureau of Public Affairs, PR 121.

(29) Alker, Bloomfield, and Choucri, Analyzing Global Interdependence, p. 3.

(30) See United Nations Department of Economic and Social Affairs, Multinational Corporations in World Development, pp. 116-17.

(31) Ibid., pp. 108-15 provide details.

(32) Ibid., pp. 106-108.

(33) Ibid., pp. 111-13.

CHAPTER 2

(1) "What you see depends on where you sit" and "Where you stand depends on where you sit" are maxims developed in the literature on bureaucratic politics in foreign policy making, but are applicable to many other situations as well.

(2) United Nations Department of Economic and Social Affairs, Multinational Corporations in World Development, p. 54 and table 42.

(3) See Jack N. Behrman, National Interests and the Multinational Enterprise (Englewood Cliffs, N.J.: Prentice-Hall, 1970), pp. 93-98.

(4) United Nations Economic and Social Council, Transnational Corporations in World Development: A Re-examination, p. 85.

(5) United Nations Department of Economic and Social Affairs, Multinational Corporations in World Development, p. 54.

(6) Tied purchases are required acquisitions of goods or services including technology which an affiliate has to make from the parent company or from another affiliate.

(7) For details see G.C. Hufbauer and F.M. Adler, Overseas Manufacturing Investment and the Balance of Payments (Washington, D.C.: U.S. Department of Commerce, 1968); and Paul P. Streeter and Sanjaya Lall, Summary of Findings of Private Foreign Manufacturing Investment in Six Developing Countries (Geneva: UNCTAD, May 1973).

(8) Ronald Muller, "Poverty is the Product," Foreign Policy, Winter 1973-74, pp. 71-102, especially 78-81 and citations therein.

(9) See R.W. Cox, "Labor and Transnational Relations," International Organization 25 (Summer 1971): 554-84, on 572.

(10) See Robert D.A. Shaw, "Foreign Investment and Global Labor," Columbia Journal of World Business 6 (July-August 1971): 52-62.

(11) See Richard J. Barnet and Ronald E. Muller, Global Reach (New York: Simon and Schuster, 1974), p. 138.

(12) Henry Schwamm and Dimitri Germidis, Code of Conduct for Multinational Companies Issues and Positions (Brussels: European Center for Study and Information on MNCs, 1977), p. 17.

(13) E.F. Kolde, International Business Enterprise (Englewood Cliffs: N.J.: Prentice-Hall, 1968), p. 278.

(14) United Nations Economic and Social Council, Transnational Corporations in World Development: A Re-examination, p. 81 and citations in note 155.

(15) See Behrman, National Interests and the Multinational Enterprise, pp. 23-26.

(16) Kolde, International Business Enterprise, p. 280.

(17) For example see Behrman, National Interests and the Multinational Enterprise, pp. 23-26.

(18) See Barnet and Muller, Global Reach, pp. 168-72.

(19) Ibid., pp. 56-57.

(20) Ibid., pp. 135-47.

(21) Ibid., pp. 158-59.

(22) Behrman, National Interests and the Multinational Enterprise, p. 71.

(23) For a more detailed discussion of this subject see Deena R. Khatkhate, "Management in Developing Countries," Finance and Development (Nov. 3, 1971) pp. 8-14, especially pp. 10-12.

(24) Charles T. Goodsell, American Corporations and Peruvian Politics (Cambridge, Mass.: Harvard University Press, 1974), pp. 95-106.

(25) Ibid., p. 99.

(26) This clause refers to contracts between the government of a state (host state) and an alien subject, perhaps an MNC, in which the alien subject agrees that any disputes that might arise out of the contract are to be decided by the state's national courts in accordance with national law and are not to give rise to any international reclamation or intervention by the alien's home government. The United States and many other countries have refused the applicability of the Calvo Clause to the extent that it impinges on the right of every state under international law to protect its citizens. See Charles G. Fenwick, International Law, 4th ed. (New York: Appleton-Century-Crofts, 1965), pp. 350-52.

CHAPTER 3

(1) United Nations Department of Economic and Social Affairs, The Impact of Multinational Corporations on Development and on International Relations (E/5500/Rev. 1., ST/ESA/6), 1974, p. 3. (Hereafter referred to as The Report.)

(2) For a complete list of the Group of Twenty Eminent Persons see ibid., p. 21.

(3) A significant study prepared by the International Labour Office was entitled Multinational Enterprises and Social Policy (Studies and Reports New Series no. 79), 1973. The UNCTAD studies will be discussed in subsequent chapters.

(4) See for example, The Acquisition of Technology from Multinational Corporations by Developing Countries (E.74.II.A.7); and The Impact

of Multinational Corporations on Development and International Relations: Technical Papers: Taxation (E.74.II.A.6).

(5) The Report, p. 25.

(6) This is acknowledged by the authors of The Report in a footnote. It defends the use of the term "corporations" because it has been utilized in the constituent ECOSOC resolution of 1972.

(7) See Raymond Vernon, "Economic Sovereignty at Bay," Foreign Affairs 47, no. 1 (October 1968): 110-22; and Howard V. Perlmutter, "Attitudinal Patterns in Joint Decision Making in Multinational Firm-Nation State Relationships" in International Decision-Making ed. M.F. Tuite, M. Radnor, and R. Chisholm, (Chicago: Aldine Publishing Co., 1972), pp. 4-5.

(8) For example, Jonathan F. Galloway, "Multinational Enterprises as World-Wide Interest Groups" (Paper delivered at the Annual Meeting of the American Political Science Association, September 1970); and J.N. Behrman, "The Multinational Enterprise: Its Initiatives and Governmental Reactions," (mimeographed, March 1971). See also Yair Aharon, "On the Definition of a Multinational Corporation," Quarterly Review of Economics and Business (August 1971), pp. 27-37; and Barnet and Muller, Global Reach, pp. 17-18.

(9) The Report, p. 26.

(10) See Summary of the Hearings Before the Group of Eminent Persons to Study the Impact of Multinational Corporations on Development and on International Relations (New York: United Nations, 1974).

(11) Robert Gilpin, "The Political Economy of the Multinational Corporations: Three Contrasting Perspectives," American Political Science Review, 70 (March 1976): 184-91.

(12) Ibid., p. 188.

(13) Ibid., p. 190.

(14) See Werner J. Feld, "The Utility of the EEC Experience for Eastern Europe," Journal of Common Market Studies 8 (March 1970): 236-61.

(15) The Report, pp. 36-42.

(16) United Nations salaries for all ranks of employees seem to exceed appreciably those paid by national governments and private industry. See International Herald Tribune, May 24, 1976, which quotes an ambassador stationed in Geneva, Switzerland, as saying: "Never have so many done so little for so much."

(17) United States Department of State, Bureau of Public Affairs, Office of Media Services, Results of the Seventh Special Session of the U.N. General Assembly, September 1-6, 1975 (Publication 8831), 8831), p. 1.

(18) See Charles T. Goodsell, American Corporations and Peruvian Politics, pp. 87-106. See also the Department of State News Release, March 5, 1976, entitled International Problems of Bribery.

(19) Sicco Mansholt, a member of the group, recommended that the sanctions imposed in accordance with due process of law of the host country may include expropriation without compensation. (The Report, p. 46.)

(20) The Report, p. 46.

(21) Ibid., p. 47.

(22) Ibid., p. 104-15.

(23) See for example, United Nations Conference on Trade and Development, Transfer of Technology (TD/106), November 10, 1971, and Walter A. Chudson, The International Transfer of Commercial Technology to Developing Countries (UNITAR Research Report no. 13), 1971, and a series of related UNITAR research reports; also United Nations Conference on Trade and Development, Guidelines for the Study of the Transfer of Technology to Developing Countries (3.72.II.D.19), December 1972.

(24) Resolution 3201 (S-VI) and 3362 (S-VII).

(25) The Report, p. 89.

(26) With respect to taxation, see ibid., pp. 91-94.

(27) Because of space limitations, we have examined only those recommendations that appeared to have major significance.

(28) The Report, p. 35.

(29) Ibid., p. 8.

(30) Ibid.

(31) The 1979 membership list is as follows: Algeria, Argentina, Benin, Brazil, Canada, Colombia, Cuba, Federal Republic of Germany, France, Fiji, German Democratic Republic, Ghana, India, Indonesia, Iran, Iraq, Italy, Ivory Coast, Jamaica, Japan, Kenya, Kuwait, Madagascar, Mexico, Netherlands, Nigeria, Pakistan, Panama, Peru, Poland, Romania, Spain, Surinam, Swaziland, Sweden, Switzerland, Thailand, Turkey, Tunisia, Uganda, USSR, United Kingdom, United States, Venezuela, Yugoslavia, Zaire, and Zambia.

(32) The Report, p. 36.

(33) Ibid., p. 88.

CHAPTER 4

(1) The Sixth Special Session promulgated the Declaration and Action Programs for establishing a New International Economic Order, and the 29th General Session resolution dealt with the Charter of Economic Rights and Duties of States.

(2) For details see United Nations Commission on Transnational Corporations, Report on the First Session, 17-28 March 1975 (E/5665/E/C,10/6), 1975 Annexes 1-3.

(3) Ibid., p. 7-13.

(4) Department of State Memorandum of June 1, 1975, on Current Status of International Activities of TNEs. A summarized list of positions and concerns of the Group of "77" and the Western developed countries is found in chapter 5, in which the issues and controversies and their bearing on the development of a code of conduct are discussed in detail.

(5) In-depth studies on the following specific subjects in all their aspects were either in process or were to be initiated: (1) the impact of activities of transnational corporations on the balance of payments of developing countries and others; (2) the service sector, including banking, insurance, shipping, and tourism; (3) the implications of investment by transnational corporations on employment in both home and host countries; (4) the extent to which investment and production by domestic enterprises, who are their competitors, suppliers, or customers; (5) extractive, food and beverages, and pharmaceutical industries (case studies); (6) obstacles to strengthening the negotiating capacity of governments in their relations with multinational corporations; (7) measures adopted by governments nationally and regionally to strengthen their negotiating capacity in their relations with transnational corporations, and lessons to be learned therefrom; (8) measures adopted by host countries to strengthen the competitive position of national enterprises vis-a-vis multinational corporations; (9) the activities of multinational corporations in southern Africa and the extent of their collaboration with the illegal regimes in that area, taking fully into account work done by the relevant bodies of the United Nations. In addition, the IRC is carrying on continuing studies on the corrupt practices of MNCs and a continuing review of research on activities of MNCs.

(6) For details see United Nations Commission on Transnational Corporations, Report on the Second Session, 1-12 March 1976 (E/5782, E/C.10/16), pp. 10-16.

(7) Ibid., Annex IV, pp. 26-34 and 23-25.

(8) The CTC Reporter, no. 2 (June 1977): 9-12. Regional meetings on the code had been held earlier in New Delhi (for the Asian countries) in August 1976 and for the African countries in Addis Ababa in January 1977.

(9) Ibid., p. 3.

(10) United Nations Commission on Transnational Corporations, <u>Report on the Resumed Second Session and the Third Session, 3 March and 25 April-6 May 1977</u>, Supplement no. 5 (E/5986.E/C,10/32), p. 13.

(11) Ibid.

(12) <u>The CTC Reporter</u>, no. 5 (September 1978): 3.

(13) Ibid., p. 5.

(14) Ibid., p. 3.

(15) <u>The CTC Reporter</u>, no. 4 (April 1978): 68.

CHAPTER 5

(1) See Schwamm and Germidis, <u>Codes of Conduct for Multinational Corporations</u>, pp. 7-8.

(2) Ibid., pp. 9-10.

(3) United Nations Commission on Transnational Corporations, <u>Text of an Annotated Outline on a Code of Conduct</u> (E/C.10/AC2/3), January 19, 1978.

(4) United Nations Commission on Transnational Corporations, <u>Text of an Annotated Outline on a Code of Conduct</u>, Working Paper no. 1, March 24, 1978.

(5) <u>The CTC Reporter</u>, no. 4 (April 1978): 6.

(6) United Nations Commission on Transnational Corporations, <u>Transnational Corporations: Code of Conduct, Formulations by the Chairman</u> (E/C.10/AC2/8), December 13, 1978. They are reproduced fully in Appendix A.

(7) United Nations Commission on Transnational Corporations, Working Paper no. 5, January 8, 1979.

(8) United Nations Economic and Social Council, Document E/C.10/46, April 3, 1979, p. 11.

(9) Paragraph 57 stresses that intergovernmental cooperation is essential in encouraging the positive contributions that MNCs can make to economic and social progress and in alleviating difficulties that may arise from MNC activities.

(10) Commission on Transnational Corporations, Working Paper no. 7, February22, 1979.

CHAPTER 6

(1) See Wall Street Journal, November 14 and 17, 1975, "Fiasco in Italy," and "Greese or Grit?" p. 1 in respective issues. Whether the enactment of strict United States disclosure laws on foreign bribes paid by American corporations will be an effective means to halt corruption overseas will have to be determined in the years to come. See the "Foreign Corrupt Practices Act" of 1977 (Public Law 95-123, December 19, 1977).

(2) For the text of the paper see United Nations Economic and Social Council, Document E/AC.64/L1, February 2, 1977.

(3) For details see United Nations Economic and Social Council, Document E/AC.64/L2, February 10, 1977.

(4) The CTC Reporter 1, no. 4 (April 1978): 7. See also The CTC Reporter 1, no. 2 (June 1977): 13 for additional details.

(5) See United Nations Commission on Trade and Development, Documents TD/B/C.6/AC.1/L.1/Rev. 1, May 16, 1975, and TD/B/C.6/AC.1/L.6, November 28, 1975 (for Brazilian draft) and TD/B/C.6/AC.1/L.2, May 5, 1975, and TD/B/C.6/AC.1/L.5, November 24, 1975 (for the Japanese proposals).

(6) Document TX/190, December 31, 1975, p. 1.

(7) Document TD/L.112, May 27, 1976, TD/B/C.6/AC.3/2, June 28, 1977, and TD/B/C.6/AC.3/3, June 29, 1977.

(8) Document TD/B/C.6/AC.1/L.6, pp. 1-4.

(9) For details see United Nations Commission on Trade and Development, Trade and Development Board, Report of the Second Ad Hoc Group of Experts on Restrictive Business Practices, October 20-24, 1975 (TD/B/C.2/AC.5/R.1), November 10, 1975, and Document TD/B/C.6/AC.1/L.1/Rev. 1, May 16, 1975, p. 9.

(10) Document TD/B/C.6/AC.1/L.5, November 24, 1975, pp. 7-8.

(11) United States Department of State, Bureau of Public Affairs, Results of the Seventh Special Session of the United Nations General Assembly, September 1-16, 1975, p. 6.

(12) Document TX/L.128, May 29, 1976.

(13) For details see United Nations, Council on Trade and Development, Document TD/L.111, May 27, 1976.

(14) United States Department of State, Bureau of Public Affairs, UNCTAD IV: Expanding Cooperation for Global Development, May 6, 1976, pp. 9, 10, 11.

(15) Document TD/L.111, p. 7.

(16) Ibid.

(17) Document TD/L.112, p. 3.

(18) United Nations Economic and Security Council, Document E/C 10/AC.2/5, July 18, 1978, pp. 11-12.

(18a) Ibid, p. 8.

(19) Ibid., p. 12.

(20) See United Nations Council on Trade and Development, Document TD/CODE TOT/10, December 22, 1978, Annex I, pp. 1-10.

(21) Ibid., pp. 11-18.

(22) Document E/C 10/AC.2/5, p. 5.

(23) Ibid., p. 6.

(24) Ibid., p. 9.

(25) Ibid., p. 10.

(26) Ibid., p. 11.

(27) United States Department of State, Bureau of Public Affairs, Results of the Seventh Special Session of the U.N. General Assembly, p. 6.

(28) Document E/C 10/AC.2/5, p. 20.

(29) For more details see Schwamm and Germidis, Codes of Conduct for Multinational Corporations, pp. 25-27.

(30) For views of employers and labor union representatives, see ibid., pp. 28-30.

(31) Document E/C 10/AC.2/5, pp. 21-28.

(32) For the full text of the Declaration, see Document E/C.10/AC.2/3, annex II.

(33) United Nations Commission on Transnational Corporations, Conference Room Paper no. 15, March 13, 1979, provides the text of the statement.

(34) United Nations Economic and Social Council, Working Paper no. 9, March 2, 1979.

CHAPTER 7

(1) United Nations Economic and Social Council, Quoted in Transnational Corporations in World Development: A Re-examination, p. 161.

(2) Ibid., p. 160.

(3) See also chapter 1, supra.

(4) Document E/C.10/46, April 3, 1979, p. 12.

(5) See also Document E/C.10/AC.2/9, December 1978, p. 25.

(6) Ibid., pp. 26-32.

(7) See Werner J. Feld and Lewis B. Kilbourne, "The U.N. Bureaucracy: Growth and Diversity," International Review of Administrative Science 43, no. 4 (1977): 321-33.

(8) Minutes of the Meeting of the Working Group on UN/OECD Investment Undertaking, January 23, 1979, p. 4.

(9) Document E/C.10/46, April 3, 1979, p. 7. See also CTC Working Paper No. 6, February 22, 1979.

(10) Document E/C.10/46, p. 7.

(11) Ibid., p. 8. Some delegates mentioned a period of five years which seems reasonable.

CHAPTER 8

(1) International Chamber of Commerce, Guidelines for International Investment (Paris, October 1974), p. 5. Hereinafter referred to as ICC Guidelines.

(2) Ibid., p. 6.

(3) See ibid., Section I for details.

(4) Ibid., Section II.

(5) Ibid., Section III.

(6) Ibid., Section IV.

(7) Ibid., Section V.

(8) Ibid., Section VI.

(9) Ibid., p. 20.

(10) For details see Ibid., Section VII.

(11) For details see International Chamber of Commerce, Guide to ICC Arbitration (Paris, 1972).

(12) "Guidelines for Multinational Enterprises," Annex to the Declaration of 21st June 1976 by Governments of OECD Member Countries on International Investment and Multinational Enterprises. Major parts of these Guidelines are presented in Appendix B.

(13) Ibid., p. 12.

(14) See note 5, chapter 3 of this work.

(15) "Guidelines for Multinational Enterprises," p. 12.

(16) Ibid., p. 14.

(17) Ibid., p. 15

(18) Ibid., p. 16-17.

(19) Ibid., p. 17.

(20) Minutes of the Meeting of the Working Group on UN/OECD Investment Undertakings, March 9, 1979, pp. 3-4.

(21) Ibid.

(22) Minutes of the Meeting of the Working Group on UN/OECD Investment Undertakings, January 23, 1979, pp. 4-5.

(23) Minutes of the March 9 Meeting, pp. 2-3.

CHAPTER 9

(1) United Nations Council on Trade and Development, Document TD/L.128, Annex B/78, May 29, 1976.

(2) For a full background on these efforts see UNCTAD Documents TD/B/C.6/AC.3/2 and 3/3 containing reports respectively on The Revision of the Paris Convention for the Protection of Industrial Property and The Impact of Trademarks on the Development Process of Developing Countries.

(3) The Report, pp. 115-40.

(4) Ibid., pp. 53-54.

(5) See for example, ibid., p. 139.

(6) The reasons for differences are partly ideological (e.g. Scandinavian countries) and partly economic (e.g., Greece, Portugal). See Schwamm and Germidis, Codes of Conduct for Multinational Corporations, p. 67.

(7) United States State Department Communication, Current Status of International Activities Relating to Transnational Enterprises (TNEs) As of November 1978, (mimeographed) p. 2.

(8) Gulf Oil Corporation and Coca Cola are other examples of firms that have instituted their own code of ethics. For comprehensive discussion of this issue see Clarence Walton, ed. The Ethics of Corporate Conduct (Englewood Cliffs, N.J.: Prentice-Hall, 1979). For an interesting analysis see "Corporate Guidelines," CTC Reporter 1, no. 5 (September 1978): 16-32.

(9) United Nations Economic and Social Council, Document E/C.10/8 and Add. 1, January 12 and 26, 1976, respectively.

(10) United Nations Economic and Social Council, Document E/5592, October 21, 1974, p. 8.

(11) For details see ECOSOC Document E/C.10/8, p. 12, and Transnational Corporations in World Development: A Re-examination, pp. 182-89.

(12) Document E/C.10/8, pp. 9-15.

(13) Ibid., pp. 15-16.

(14) See New York Times, March 24, 1979, p. 25; and (New Orleans) Times Picayune, November 9, 1978, p. 16.

(15) See David A. Jodice, "The Politics of Expropriation: Sources of Change in Latin American Regimes for Foreign Investment in Natural Resource Extraction, 1968-1976" (Paper delivered at the ISA Convention, March 21-25, 1979).

(16) See Raymond Vernon, Storm over the Multinationals (Cambridge, Mass.: Harvard University Press, 1973), p. 197.

(17) Ibid., pp. 196-97.

(18) For additional details and examples, see Franklin B. Weinstein, "Underdevelopment and Efforts to Control Multinational Corporations," in Transnational Corporations and World Order, ed. George Modelski (San Francisco, Calif.: W.H. Foreman, 1978), pp. 338-46.

(19) Ibid.

(20) The Report, p. 133.

(21) See Wall Street Journal, September 22, 1975, p. 22, and October 9, 1975, p. 14.

(22) For a breakdown of these expropriations see Transnational Corporations in World Development: A Re-examination, Tables III-28, III-29, and III-30, on pp. 232-34. The most expropriations took place in Algeria, Angola, Egypt, Ethiopia, Indonesia, Sri Lanka, Sudan, Tanzania, and Uganda. All economic sectors suffered, not only raw materials as is frequently assumed. See also Theodore Moran, "Multinational Corporations and Dependency: A Dialogue for Dependistas and Non-Dependistas," International Organization 32, no. 1 (Winter 1978): 79-100.

(23) See Wall Street Journal, December 12, 1976, p. 1, and February 27, 1979, p. 27.

(24) See Wall Street Journal, February 8, 1978, p. 12.

(25) See the speech of Secretary Vance in Seattle, Washington, March 1979. Bureau of Public Affairs, The Secretary of State, March 30, 1979.

(26) See Vernon, Storm Over the Multinationals, pp. 212, 215, where he lists other examples.

(27) Perlmutter and Saghafi-nejad, "Process or Product," p. 37.

(28) Ibid., pp. 38-39.

(29) Pierre Uri, <u>Development Without Dependence</u> (New York: Praeger, 1976), pp. 162-63.

Appendix A:
Transnational Corporations:
Code of Conduct;
Formulations by the
Chairman (E/C.10/AC.2/8)

COMMISSION ON TRANSNATIONAL CORPORATIONS
Intergovernmental Working Group on a Code of Conduct
Sixth session, 8-19 January 1979

INTRODUCTORY NOTE

This paper is in response to a request by the Intergovernmental Working Group at its fifth session. It should be regarded as an attempt to consolidate the discussions of the Intergovernmental Working Group so far. The Chairman is responsible for its form and contents and it does not commit delegations in any way.

Since the legal nature of the Code still has to be discussed by the Working Group, and the imperative scope of formulations related to the activities of transnational corporations as well as the treatment of transnational corporations should not be prejudged at this stage, the word "should", wherever appropriate, is used throughout the formulations without prejudice to a final agreement on the legal nature of Code.

One exception to this principle is made. Agreement among Governments on intergovernmental co-operation is considered to be of fundamental importance to ensure the effectiveness of the Code of Conduct. This idea has received broad support in the Intergovernmental Working Group. In dealing with intergovernmental co-operation in a separate section of the Code, the proper location of which has to be determined later, the word "agree" appears to be the most appropriate.

ACTIVITIES OF TRANSNATIONAL CORPORATIONS

A. General and political

Respect for national sovereignty and observance of domestic laws, regulations and administrative practices

1. As set forth in this Code, transnational corporations should recognize and respect the national sovereignty of the countries in which they operate as well as the right of each State to exercise full permanent sovereignty over its resources and economic activities within its territory.

2. Transnational corporations should observe the laws, regulations and adminisrative practices of the countries in which they operate.

3. Transnational corporations should respect the right of each State to regulate and monitor the activities of their entities operating within its territory.

Adherence to economic goals and development objectives policies and priorities

4. Consistent with the need to maintain the viability of their operations, transnational corporations should take effective measures to ensure that their activities are compatible with and make a positive contribution toward the achievement of the economic goals and established development objectives of the countries in which they operate. To this effect transnational corporations should support the development efforts of the countries in which they operate, particularly developing countries, and participate effectively in these efforts at the national level, and where appropriate, at the regional level within the framework of regional integration programmes. In this context, they should consult and co-operate, as appropriate, with governmental authorities regarding ways of maximizing their contributions to the development process and of establishing mutually beneficial relations with these countries.

5. Transnational corporations should as all parties to contracts freely entered into, respect and adhere to such contracts. In the absence of contractual clauses providing for review or renegotiation, transnational corporations should respond positively to requests for review or renegotiation of contracts concluded with Governments or governmental agencies in circumstances marked by duress, or clear inequality between the parties, or where the conditions upon which such a contract was based have fundamentally changed, causing thereby unforeseen major distortions in the relations between the parties and thus rendering the contract unfair or oppressive to either of the parties. Aiming at ensuring fairness to all parties concerned, review or renegotiation in such situations should be undertaken in accordance with applicable legal principles and generally recognized legal practices.

Adherence to socio-cultural objectives and values

6. Transnational corporations should respect the social and cultural objectives and values of the countries in which they operate. To this end, transnational corporations should consult with Governments with a view to avoiding that their practices, products or services cause distortions in basic cultural patterns or have socio-cultural effects, considered undesirable by the countries concerned, beyond those which necessarily accompany economic development and the introduction or generation of new technologies.

Respect for human rights and fundamental freedoms

7. Transnational corporations should respect human rights and fundamental freedoms.

8. In their employment practices transnational corporations should not discriminate on the basis of race, colour, sex, religion, language, social origin, or political and other opinions. Transnational corporations should apply this principle without prejudice to government policies designed to extend equality of opportunity.

9. Non-collaboration by transnational corporations with racist minority regimes in southern Africa.*

Non-interference in internal political affairs

10. Transnational corporations should not interfere in the internal political affairs of countries in which they operate by resorting to subversive activities aimed at influencing the political and social systems in these countries.

11. Acting as good corporate citizens in the countries in which they operate, transnational corporations should abstain from activities of a political nature which are inconsistent with domestic legislation or established practice in these countries.

Non-interference in intergovernmental relations

12. Transnational corporations should not interfere in affairs which are properly the concern of Governments.

13. Transnational corporations should not act as instruments for the advancement of the foreign policy of Governments, unless they operate in accordance with intergovernmental co-operative arrangements involving the countries in which they operate or behave in harmony with

---

* The formulation of a text on the basis of this common element will be made after the Intergovernmental Working Group has had a full discussion on the issue.

concerted actions of the international community.

14. Transnational corporations, in pursuing their corporate interests, should not request Governments to act on their behalf in any manner that exceeds normal diplomatic representation or other regular intergovernmental communication and in particular in any manner that amounts to the use of coercive measures of an economic and political character.

15. Transnational corporations should, in accordance with generally accepted international standards, exhaust means provided by local law in host countries in which they operate or other agreed means for resolving disputes, before seeking diplomatic protection from their home Governments.

Abstention from corrupt practices*

16.

B. Economic, financial and social

Ownership and control

17. Transnational corporations should allocate decision making among their entities so as to enable these entities to act as good corporate citizens and to contribute to the economic and social development of the countries in which they operate.

18. The various entities of transnational corporations should co-operate with one another to help meet effectively the requirements established by the countries in which they operate.

19. Transnational corporations should co-operate with Governments and nationals of the countries in which they operate in furthering national objectives for local equity participation.

20. Transnational corporations should ensure that the control shared by local partners as determined by equity or contractual terms in non-equity arrangements can be effectively exercised.

21. In implementing their personnel policies, transnational corporations should give priority to the employment and promotion of nationals of host countries at all levels of management and direction with a view to enhancing their effective participation in the decision-making process of local entities.

22. Transnational corporations should contribute to the managerial training of nationals of host countries and facilitate their employment

---

* The formulation of a text will be made after the work in this field is further advanced.

at all levels of management of the transnational corporation as a whole.

Balance of payments and financing

23. With full regard to the policy objectives of the countries in which they operate, particularly those of developing countries, transnational corporations should, while maintaining the viability of their entities, contribute to the promotion, and to the extent possible the diversification, of exports from these countries as well as to an increased utilization of goods, services and other resources of such countries.

24. Transnational corporations should be responsive to requests by Governments in host countries, particularly developing countries, concerning the phasing, over a period of time to be agreed upon, of the repatriation of capital in case of disinvestment, or remittances of accumulated profits, dividends or intracorporate payments, when the size and timing of such transfers would aggravate serious balance-of-payments problems of such countries.

25. In managing their short-term capital transactions, transnational corporations should not, contrary to generally accepted commercial practice, defer or advance current intracorporate payments in a manner that would increase currency instability, thereby aggravating serious balance-of-payments problems of the countries in which they operate.

26. Transnational corporations should, in their intracorporate activities, refrain from imposing, contrary to established development objectives of the countries in which they operate and beyond generally accepted commercial practice, restrictions on their entities regarding the transfer of goods, services or funds, which would adversely affect the balance of payments of such countries.

27. When using capital markets of host countries, particularly for medium and long-term financing, transnational corporations should, consistent with the policies of such countries, refrain from activities which would adversely affect the functioning of such markets, particularly by restricting substantially the availability of funds to domestic enterprises. When issuing, in accordance with governmental policies, shares to nationals of host countries in order to increase local equity participation in entities operating in such countries, transnational corporations should consult with the Governments concerned on the effects of such transactions on the local capital markets.

28. Transnational corporations should consult and co-operate with Governments in countries in which they operate, with a view to alleviating problems pertaining to balance of payments and financing of undertakings in such countries and to contributing to the achievement of national goals in this respect.

Transfer pricing

In their intracorporate transactions transnational corporations should not use pricing principles, which, contrary to national legislation and policies, serve to modify the tax base on which their entities are assessed, avoid exchange controls or adversely affect competition, technological development or employment and social conditions in the countries, in which they operate.

30. In their intracorporate transactions transnational corporations should use pricing policies based on international market prices, or in the absence of such prices, the "arm's length" principle.

31. Under conditions and safeguards set forth in this Code, transnational corporations should disclose to the public the principles applied by them in transfer pricing and supply to Governmental authorities all relevant information related to transfer pricing.

Taxation*

32.

Competition and restrictive business practices*

33.

Transfer of technology*

34.

Employment and labour**

35.

Consumer protection

36. In accordance with national laws, regulations, administrative practices and policies of the countries in which they operate and relevant international standards, transnational corporations should perform their operations in a manner that does not impose dangers to the health and safety of consumers or bring about variations in the quality of products in each market to the detriment of consumers.

37. Under conditions and safeguards set forth in this Code, transnational corporations should supply to the authorities of the countries in which they operate all relevant information concerning:

- features of their products and services which may affect the health and safety of consumers;

- prohibitions, restrictions, warnings and other regulatory measures imposed in other countries on grounds of health and

---

* The formulations under this heading will be made after further discussions of the Intergovernmental Working Group, taking into consideration relevant work in other bodies.

** A tentative formulation under this heading appears in a working paper prepared by the Centre on Transnational Corporations as requested at the fifth session of the Intergovernmental Working Group.

safety protection on products which they produce or market or propose to produce or market in the countries concerned;

- experimental uses and related aspects of products which they propose to produce or market in the countries concerned.

38. Transnational corporations should disclose to the public in the countries in which they operate all appropriate information on the contents and possible hazardous effects of the products they produce or market in the countries concerned by means of proper labelling, informative and accurate advertising and other appropriate methods.

39. Transnational corporations should co-operate with the Governments of the countries in which they operate and with international organizations with a view to developing and promoting national and international standards for the protection of the health and safety of consumers, and meeting the basic needs of consumers.

Environmental protection

40. In accordance with national laws, regulations, administrative practices and policies of the countries in which they operate as well as relevant international standards, transnational corporations, in performing their activities, should protect and improve the environment and make efforts to develop and apply adequate technologies for this purpose.

41. Under conditions and safeguards set forth in this Code, transnational corporations should supply to the authorities of the countries in which they operate, all relevant information concerning:

- features of their products or processes which may harm the environment and the measures and costs required to avoid harmful effects;

- prohibitions, restrictions, warnings and other regulatory measures imposed in other countries, on grounds of protection of the environment, on products and processes which they have introduced or intend to introduce in the countries concerned.

42. Transnational corporations should co-operate with Governments of the countries in which they operate and with international organizations in environmental protection activities with a view to developing and promoting national and international standards in this field.

C. Disclosure of information

43. Transnational corporations should, within reasonable time-limits and on a regular basis, but at least annually, provide to the public in the countries in which they operate, clear and comprehensible information designed to improve understanding of the structure, activities and policies of the transnational corporation as a whole.

Such information should supplement information required by national laws, regulations and administrative practices and be provided in a consolidated form. It should include financial as well as non-financial items, such as the structure of the transnational corporation, the main activities of its entities, the operating results and sales, significant new investment, the sources and uses of funds, employment, the research and development expendicture, the transfer pricing policies applied and the accounting principles used in compiling and consolidating the information.*

In providing information, transnational corporations should have particular regard to the significance of their operations for the countries concerned, irrespective of the relative importance of such operations for the transnational corporation as a whole.

The information should be broken down by geographical area, country of operation and major line of business as appropriate. The method of breakdown as well as the detail of information required is to be determined by the nature, scale and interrelationship of the transnational corporations' operations in various countries, the effects of disclosure on the transnational corporations' competitive position and the costs involved in producing information.**

44. Transnational corporations should supply to the authorities of the countries in which they operate, upon request, and on a regular basis as specified by Governments, all information required for legislative and administrative purposes relevant to their entities in the countries concerned and specifically needed to assess the performance of such entities.

Transnational corporations should, subject to relevant national legislation of all countries concerned, supply such information held in other countries, in order to enable governments requiring information to

----

* The listing of items should be regarded as illustrative. All these items have been referred to by delegates. The discussions of the Inter-governmental Working Group so far, however, does not permit any conclusions as to what specific formulations could meet with the approval of the Intergovernmental Working Group. Furthermore, the Ad Hoc Intergovernmental Working Group of Experts on International Standards of Accounting and Reporting, the mandate of which explicitly refers to the Code of Conduct, may provide guidance in this respect.

** The ultimate formulation of these qualifications obviously will depend on the specificity given to the items of information required.

obtain a true and fair view of the operations of the transnational corporation as a whole.*

TREATMENT OF TRANSNATIONAL CORPORATIONS

A. General treatment of transnational corporations by the countries in which they operate

45. The countries in which transnational corporatios operate determine the role that such corporations may be called to play in economic and social development. This Code does not affect the right of countries to regulate the establishment or entry of transnational corporations, including prohibitions or limitations on the extent of foreign presence in specified sectors.

46. With a view to creating mutually beneficial relations, transnational corporations should be given fair and equitable treatment by the countries in which they operate, in accordance with national laws, regulations and administrative practices as well as international obligations to which States have freely subscribed.

47. Consistent with national needs to maintain public order and to protect national security, transnational corporations should be accorded the same treatment under national laws, regulations and administrative practices of countries in which they operate as that accorded to domestic enterprises, in situations where the operations of transnational corporations are comparable to those of domestic enterprises.

48. Clarity and stability of national policies, laws, regulations and administrative practices significantly affecting the activities of transnational corporations are important elements in creating conditions by which mutually beneficial relations can be promoted. When, in the light of evolving circumstances, changes are deemed necessary by the Governments of countries in which transnational corporations operate, the changes should be made with proper regard to the legitimate expectations of such corporations and the impact on their activities in the countries concerned.

49. Unless they operate in accordance with intergovernmental co-operative arrangements involving the countries in which they operate or behave in harmony with concerted actions of the international community, transnational corporations should not be used by any Government as instruments for the attainment of foreign policy objectives.

50. Government action toward other countries on behalf of transnational corporations is subject to generally accepted international standards

---

* The International Working Group has yet to decide whether standards on information to the employees in addition to those contained in the ILO Declaration of Principles are required in the context of this Code.

regarding exhaustion of local remedies, diplomatic representation and protection, and the submission of international legal claims, and should not amount to the use of coercive measures of an economic or political character.

51. Information supplied by transnational corporations in confidence to the authorities of the countries in which they operate should be subject to appropriate safeguards regarding its confidentiality in order to protect the position of the corporations concerned in relation to their competitors.*

B. Nationalization and compensation

52. In the exercise of their sovereignty, States have the right, acting in the public interest, to nationalize property in their territory. Fair and equitable treatment of transnational corporations by the countries in which they operate includes payment of just compensation in the event of nationalization or other taking of their property, such Government action being undertaken under due process of law, in accordance with national laws, regulations and administrative practices without discrimination between enterprises in comparable situations and with full regard to international obligations and contractual undertakings to which States have freely subscribed.**

C. Jurisdiction

53. Entities of transnational corporations are subject to the jurisdiction of the countries in which they operate.

54. Disputes between a State and a transnational corporation, which are not amicably settled between the parties, are subject to the jurisdiction of the courts and other authorities of that State and are to be submitted to them, except for disputes which the State has agreed to settle by arbitration or by other methods of dispute settlement.

55. The validity of clauses providing for selection of applicable law or of the forum for settlement of disputes or for commercial arbitration in contracts between private parties, at least one of which is an entity of a transnational corporation, is to be determined by the national law of the countries concerned.

56. Where the exercise of jurisdiction over transnational corporations and their entities by more than one State may lead to conflicts of

---

* A tentative formulation on the issue of "timely and unrestricted transfer or capital" appears in a working paper prepared by the Centre on Transnational Corporations as requested at the fifth session of the Intergovernmental Working Group.

** See annex for specific comments on this paragraph.

principles and procedures, bilaterally of multilaterally, for the avoidance or settlement of such conflicts, on the basis of respect for the interests of the States concerned and relevant international obligations, serves to improve the relations among States and between States and transnational corporations.

INTERGOVERNMENTAL CO-OPERATION*

57. Governments agree that intergovernmental co-operation on a bilateral as well as multilateral basis is essential in encouraging the positive contributions that transnational corporations can make to economic and social progress and in alleviating difficulties to which the activities of transnational corporations may give rise.

58. Governments further agree that such co-operation is necessary to ensure the effectiveness of this Code, particularly with regard to the exchange of information relevant to the various parts of the Code and the resolution of difficulties stemming from conflicting requirements or jurisdictional claims by Governments.

ANNEX

Comments on nationalization and compensation (para. 52)

1. There is considerable controversy concerning the international legal principles and rules governing compensation in case of nationalization or other taking of foreign-owned property. The text or paragraph 52 attempts to reflect the points on which there appears to be general agreement. As to other points it attempts to articulate standards, which do not seriously infringe on the basic positions of States or group of States. Several aspects of the topic are dealt with in other parts of the Code and it would serve no purpose merely to repeat those points in paragraph 52.

2. The first sentence of paragraph 52 states the general principle that States possess the sovereign right to nationalize property in their territory. Like any other right, this right may be limited by means of international agreements specifying particular modalities for its exercise (e.g., that full compensation will be granted, prior to the taking). Again like other rights, its exercise in manifest bad faith (e.g., nationalization not in the public interest but for private gain) may cause

---

* A number of suggestions were made in the Intergovernmental Working Group to the effect that the issues pertaining to intergovernmental co-operation be separated from IV. In response to those suggestions these issues are dealt with under a separate heading.

legal problems, although it is hard to imagine actual situations where a sovereign State's good faith in exercising a sovereign right may be successfully impugned.

3. While considerable controversy exists concerning the international legal principles and rules governing the award of compensation for nationalized property, it is possible to mention several points on which there seems to be fairly general agreement:

(a) Owners of property being nationalized are normally entitled to compensation, although there is no agreement as to the law (national or international) that determines the modalities of compensation;

(b) Where specific international commitments exist (e.g., in an international treaty), the modalities of compensation will be governed by them;

(c) The national law of the nationalizing country is relevant. According to one view, it is the only relevant law; international law either has no relevant rules or it provides that national law is the only law applicable.   According to another view, international law also includes certain independent standards, which override or supplement national law in order to protect the aliens affected.

4. The second sentence of paragraph 52 does not attempt to state international legal principles or rules. It describes the kind of measures concerning compensation for nationalization which would constitute "fair and equitable treatment" of transnational corporations.   Such treatment has already been dealt with in paragraph 46.   To the extent that consistent implementation of the Code of Conduct (assuming that it would include this or equivalent language) would influence state practice an ultimate impact upon international law may be assumed. But the text of paragraph 52 as such does not purport to state what international law is on the subject.

5. The elements listed in connexion with the type of compensation that would constitute "fair and equitable treatment" are similar to those frequently mentioned in discussions of legal requirements, but here they are listed in view of their contributing to "fair and equitable treatment," thus leaving unaffected whatever legal status they have.

6. The adjective "just" refers to the final outcome of the compensation process rather than to the particular methods and criteria employed. A just result is to be sought taking into account all relevant circumstances in each case.

7. The reference to "due process of law" is intended to preclude arbitrary and capricious action on the part of Governments.   While certain general principles as to what constitutes due process of law are broadly and virtually universally accepted, the specific rules concerning due process are to be found in national law regulations and administrative practices, and paragraph 52 duly refers to "national laws, regulations and administrative practices."

8. The concept of 'discrimination' involves undue differentiation both between entities of foreign transnational corporations of differing national origin and between entities of foreign-based transnational corporations and local enterprises. To make comparison possible and thereby a finding as to the presence or lack of discrimination, the enterprises involved must be in situations which are reasonably similar. In the assessment of the degree of similarity of situations, criteria such as size, origin, sector, etc. will have to be used as appropriate in each particular case.

9. The duty of States to comply with freely undertaken international obligations is self-evident and requires no explanation. Obviously, problems of interpretation may arise with respect to the scope of the international obligation or to the character of the relevant acts. These will have to be resolved by peaceful means like other disputes between States.

10. It is not the purpose of the language offered in paragraph 52 to resolve the profound and long-standing differences of opinion between States on the issue of nationalization and compensation. The goal is to present a text which will be acceptable to all States concerned and which would, at the same time, express some meaningful standards -not merely evade the issue.

Appendix B:
Guidelines for Multinational Enterprises
(OECD Document)

GUIDELINES FOR MULTINATIONAL ENTERPRISES*

1. .....

2. The common aim of the Member countries is to encourage the positive contributions which multinational enterprises can make to economic and social progress and to minimise and resolve the difficulties to which their various operations may give rise. .....

3. .....

4. Within the Organisation, the programme of co-peration to attain these ends will be a continuing, pragmatic and balanced one. It comes within the general aims of the Convention on the Organisation for Economic Co-operation and Development (OECD) and makes full use of the various specialised bodies of the Organisation, whose terms of reference already cover many aspects of the role of multinational enterprises, notably in matters of international trade and payments, competition, taxation, manpower, industrial development, science and technology. .....

5. .....

6. The guidelines set out below are recommendations jointly addressed by Member countries to multinational enterprises operating in their territories. These guidelines, which take into account the problems which can arise because of the international structure of these

---

* Annex to the Declaration of 21st June 1976 by Governments of OECD Member Countries on International Investment and Multinational Enterprises.

enterprises, lay down standards for the activities of these enterprises in the different Member countries. Observance of the guidelines is voluntary and not legally enforceable. However, they should help to ensure that the operations of these enterprises are in harmony with national policies of the countries where they operate and to strengthen the basis of mutual confidence between enterprises and States.

7. Every State has the right to prescribe the conditions under which multinational enterprises operate within its national jurisdiction, subject to international law and to the international agreements to which it has subscribed. The entities of a multinational enterprise located in various countries are subject to the laws of these countries.

8. A precise legal definition of multinational enterprises is not required for the purposes of the guidelines. These usually comprise companies or other entities whose ownership is private, state or mixed, established in different countries and so linked that one or more of them may be able to exercise a significant influence over the activities of others and, in particular, to share knowledge and resources with the others. The degree of autonomy of each entity in relation to the others varies widely from one multinational enterprise to another, depending on the nature of the links between such entities and the fields of activity concerned. For these reasons, the guidelines are addressed to the various entities within the multinational enterprise (parent companies and/or local entities) according to the actual distribution of responsibilities among them on the understanding that they will co-operate and provide assistance to one another as necessary to facilitate observance of the guidelines. The word "enterprise" as used in these guidelines refers to these various entities in accordance with their responsibilities.

9. The guidelines are not aimed at introducing differences of treatment between multinational and domestic enterprises; wherever relevant they reflect good practice for all. Accordingly, multinational and domestic enterprises are subject to the same expectations in respect of their conduct wherever the guidelines are relevant to both.

10. The use of appropriate international dispute settlement mechanisms, including arbitration, should be encouraged as a means of facilitating the resolution of problems arising between enterprises and Member countries.

11. Member countries have agreed to establish appropriate review and consultation procedures concerning issues arising in respect of the guidelines. When multinational enterprises are made subject to conflicting requirements by Member countries, the governments concerned will co-operate in good faith with a view to resolving such problems either within the Committee on International Investment and Multinational Enterprises established by the OECD Council on 21st January 1975 or through other mutually acceptable arrangements.

Having regard to the foregoing considerations, the Member countries set forth the following guidelines for multinational enterprises with the understanding that Member countries will fulfil their responsibilities to treat enterprises equitably and in accordance with international law and international agreements, as well as contractual obligations to which they have subscribed:

GENERAL POLICIES

Enterprises should

1. take fully into account established general policy objectives of the Member countries in which they operate;

2. in particular, give due consideration to those countries' aims and priorities with regard to economic and social progress, including industrial and regional development, the protection of the environment, the creation of employment opportunities, the promotion of innovation and the transfer of technology;

3. while observing their legal obligations concerning information, supply their entities with supplementary information the latter may need in order to meet requests by the authorities of the countries in which those entities are located for information relevant to the activities of those entities, taking into account legitimate requirements of business confidentiality;

4. favour close co-operation with the local community and business interests;

5. allow their component entities freedom to develop their activities and to exploit their competitive advantage in domestic and foreign markets, consistent with the need for specialisation and sound commercial practice;

6. when filling responsible posts in each country of operation, take due account of individual qualifications without discrimination as to nationality, subject to particular national requirements in this respect;

7. not render--and they should not be solicited or expected to render--any bribe or other improper benefit, direct or indirect, to any public servant or holder of public office;

8. unless legally permissible, not make contributions to candidates for public office or to political parties or other political organisations;

9. abstain from any improper involvement in local political activities.

DISCLOSURE OF INFORMATION

Enterprises should, having due regard to their nature and relative size in the economic context of their operations and to requirements of business confidentiality and to cost, publish in a form suited to improve public understanding a sufficient body of factual information on the structure, activities and policies of the enterprise as a whole, as a supplement, in so far as necessary for this purpose, to information to be disclosed under the national law of the individual countries in which they operate. To this end, they should publish within reasonable time limits, on a regular basis, but at least annually, financial statements and other pertinent information relating to the enterprise as a whole, comprising in particular:

i) the structure of the enterprise, showing the name and location of the parent company, its main affiliates, its percentage owner-ship, direct and indirect, in these affiliates, including share-holdings between them;

ii) the geographical areas where operations are carried out and the principal activities carried on therein by the parent company and the main affiliates;*

iii) the operating results and sales by geographical area and the sales in the major lines of business for the enterprise as a whole;

iv) significant new capital investment by geographical area and, as far as practicable, by major lines of business for the enterprise as a whole;

v) a statement of the sources and uses of funds by the enterprise as a whole;

vi) the average number of employees in each geographical area;

vii) research and development expenditure for the enterprise as a whole;

viii) the policies followed in respect of intra-group pricing;

ix) the accounting policies, including those on consolidation, ob-served in compiling the published information.

COMPETITION

Enterprises should, while conforming to official competition rules and established policies of the countries in which they operate,

----

* For the purposes of the guideline on disclosure of information the term "geographical area" means groups of countries or individual countries as each enterprise determines is appropriate in its particular circumstances. While no single method of grouping is appropriate for all enterprises or for all purposes, the factors to be considered by an enterprise would include the significance of operations carried out in individual countries or areas as well as the effects on its competitive-ness, geographic proximity, economic affinity, similarities in business environments and the nature, scale and degree of interrelationship of the enterprises' operations in the various countries.

1. refrain from actions which would adversely affect competition in the relevant market by abusing a dominant position of market power, by means of, for example,

   a) anti-competitive acquisitions,
   b) predatory behaviour toward competitors,
   c) unreasonable refusal to deal,
   d) anti-competitive abuse of industrial property rights,
   e) discriminatory (i.e. unreasonably differentiated) pricing and using such pricing transactions between affiliated enterprises as a means of affecting adversely competition outside these enterprises;

2. allow purchasers, distributors and licensees freedom to resell, export, purchase and develop their operations consistent with law, trade conditions, the need for specialisation and sound commercial practice;

3. refrain from participating in or otherwise purposely strengthening the restrictive effects of international or domestic cartels or restrictive agreements which adversely affect or eliminate competition and which are not generally or specifically accepted under applicable national or international legislation;

4. be ready to consult and co-operate, including the provision of information, with competent authorities of countries whose interests are directly affected in regard to competition issues or investigations. Provision of information should be in accordance with safeguards normally applicable in this field.

FINANCING

Enterprises should, in managing the financial and commercial operations of their activities, and especially their liquid foreign assets and liabilities, take into consideration the establised objectives of the countries in which they operate regarding balance of payments and credit policies.

TAXATION

Enterprises should

1. upon request of the taxation authorities of the countries in which they operate, provide, in accordance with the safeguards and relevant procedures of the national laws of these countries, the information necessary to determine correctly the taxes to be assessed in connection with their operations, including relevant information concerning their operations in other countries;

2. refrain from making use of the particular facilities available to them, such as transfer pricing which does not conform to an arm's length standard, for modifying in ways contrary to national laws the tax base on which members of the group are assessed.

EMPLOYMENT AND INDUSTRIAL RELATIONS

Enterprises should, within the framework of law, regulations and prevailing labour relations and employment practices, in each of the countries in which they operate,

1. respect the right of their employees, to be represented by trade unions and other bona fide organisations of employees, and engage in constructive negotiations, either individually or through employers' associations, with such employee organisations with a view to reaching agreements on employment conditions, which should include provisions for dealing with disputes arising over the interpretation of such agreements, and for ensuring mutually respected rights and responsibilities;

2. a) provide such facilities to representatives of the employees as may be necessary to assist in the development of effective collective agreements,

   b) provide to representatives of employees information which is needed for meaningful negotiations on conditions of employment;

3. provide to representatives of employees where this accords with local law and practice, information which enables them to obtain a true and fair view of the performance of the entity or, where appropriate, the enterprise as a whole;

4. observe standards of employment and industrial relations not less favourable than those observed by comparable employers in the host country;

5. in their operations, to the greatest extent practicable, utilise, train and prepare for upgrading members of the local labour force in co-operation with representatives of their employees and, where appropriate, the relevant governmental authorities;

6. in considering changes in their operations which would have major effects upon the livelihood of their employees, in particular in the case of the closure of an entity involving collective lay-offs or dismissals, provide reasonable notice of such changes to representatives of their employees, and where appropriate to the relevant governmental authorities, and co-operate with the employee respresentatives and appropriate governmental authorities so as to mitigate to the maximum extent practicable adverse effects;

7. implement their employment policies including hiring, discharge, pay, promotion and training without discrimination unless selectivity in respect of employee characteristics is in furtherance of established governmental policies which specifically promote greater equality of employment opportunity;

8. in the context of bona fide negotiations* with representatives of employees on conditions of employment, or while employees are exercising a right to organise, not threaten to utilise a capacity to transfer the whole or part of an operating unit from the country concerned in order to influence unfairly those negotiations or to hinder the exercise of a right to organise;

9. enable authorised representatives of their employees to conduct negotiations on collective bargaining or labour management relations issues with representatives of management who are authorised to take decisions on the matters under negotiation.

SCIENCE AND TECHNOLOGY

Enterprises should

1. endeavour to ensure that their activities fit satisfactorily into the scientific and technological policies and plans of the countries in which they operate, and contribute to the development of national scientific and technological capacities, including as far as appropriate the establishment and improvement in host countries of their capacity to innovate;

2. to the fullest extent practicable, adopt in the course of their business activities practices which permit the rapid diffusion of technologies with due regard to the protection of industrial and intellectual property rights;

3. when granting licences for the use of industrial property rights or when otherwise transferring technology do so on reasonable terms and conditions.

---

* Bona fide negotiations may include labour disputes as part of the process of negotiation. Whether or not labour disputes are so included will be determined by the law and prevailing employment practices of particular countries.

Glossary

1.	BIAC	Business and Industry Advisory Committee to OECD
2.	CIEC	Conference on International Economic Co-operation
3.	CIME	Committee on International Investment and Multi-national Enterprise
4.	CSID	World Bank's Centre for the Settlement of Investment Disputes
5.	CTC	United Nations Centre on Transnational Corporations
6.	CTN	Commission on Transnational Corporations
7.	ECOSOC	United Nations Economic and Social Council
8.	EEC	European Economic Community
9.	FAO	Food and Agriculture Organization
10.	GATT	General Agreement on Tariffs and Trade
11.	ICC	International Chamber of Commerce
12.	ICFTU	International Confederation of Free Trade Unions
13.	IMF	International Monetary Fund
14.	IGOs	Intergovernmental Organizations
15.	ILO	International Labour Organization
16.	LDCs	Less Developed Countries
17.	NICs	New Industrial Countries
18.	NIEO	New International Economic Order
18a	OAS	Organization of American States
18b	OAU	Organization of African Unity

19. OECD   Organization for Economic Co-operation and Development

20. OPEC   Organization of Petroleum Exporting Countries

21. TUAC   Trade Union Advisory Committee

22. UNCTAD   United Nations Conference on Trade and Development

23. UNESCO   United Nations Educational, Scientific, and Cultural Organization

24. UNIDO   United Nations Industrial Development Organization

25. UNITAR   United Nations Institute for Training and Research

26. WFTU   World Federation of Trade Unions

27. WIPO   World Intellectual Property Organization

Index

About the Author

WERNER J. FELD is a Professor of Political Science at the University of New Orleans. He is author of numerous publications, including Transnational Business Collaboration Among Common Market Countries (1970); Nongovernmental Forces and World Politics (1972); The European Community in World Affairs (1976); Domestic Political Realities and European Unification (with John K. Wildgen), (1976); The Foreign Policies of West European Socialist Parties (ed.) (1978); and International Relations: A Transnational Approach (1979). In addition, Dr. Feld is the author of more than 50 articles in various journals. He received a law degree from the University of Berlin and a Ph.D. in political science from Tulane University.